ecpr PRESS
classics

Series Editor: Alan Ware
University of Oxford

political
elites

Geraint Parry

with a new introduction by the author

ecpr PRESS

First published in 1969
Second impression 1970
Third impression 1971
by George Allen & Unwin Ltd

First published by the ECPR Press in 2005

The ECPR Press is the publishing imprint of the European Consortium for Political Research (ECPR), a scholarly association, which supports and encourages the training, research and cross-national cooperation of political scientists in institutions throughout Europe and beyond. The ECPR's Central Services are located at the University of Essex, Wivenhoe Park, Colchester, CO4 3SQ, UK

Typeset in Times 10pt by the ECPR Press

British Library Cataloguing in Publication Data
A catalogue record for this book is available from the British Library

ISBN 0-9547966-0-8

ecpr PRESS
classics

The ECPR Classics series is published by the ECPR Press, the publishing imprint of the European Consortium for Political Research (ECPR).

As an independent, scholarly institution, one of the ECPR's objectives is to facilitate research in political science among European universities. To that end, the ECPR has developed a strong publishing portfolio since the 1970s.

The policy to extend that portfolio by launching its own publishing imprint was discussed by the Executive Committee of the ECPR in 2002, and the decision to proceed was taken in early 2003.

It was decided that the first two series to be published under the imprint should be complementary. The ECPR Monographs series publishes major new research in all sub-disciplines of political science. The ECPR Classics series facilitates scholarly access to significant works from earlier eras of political science by re-publishing books that have been out of print. It believes this will enable contemporary students and researchers to develop their own work more effectively.

While every effort has been made to reproduce faithfully the original text, the pagination of this ECPR Classics edition differs slightly from the pagination in the original edition of the work; this follows from the decision to keep the size of page and font consistent across all titles in the series. To enable scholars to locate cited page references to the earlier edition, the original chapter pagination is stated at the beginning of the corresponding chapter in this ECPR Classics edition. The Index of this edition also includes both the original and the ECPR Classics edition page numbers for each entry.

Alan Ware
Editor, ECPR Classics and ECPR Monographs
Worcester College, Oxford University, UK

Other titles in this series:

Titles in the ECPR Monographs series:

contents

political | new introduction by the author
elites |

It is a curious experience to write a new introduction to a work composed around thirty-five years previously. There is some comfort to be drawn from such an invitation in so far as it implies that one should not be entirely embarrassed by one's early thoughts. On the other hand to embark on a substantial revision is difficult in that one's perspective inevitably changes over such a period and one would not now be starting from the same place. I have therefore preferred to let the original text speak for itself as a review of how elite studies appeared at a time when elite approaches to politics were engaged in a mixture of normative, methodological and substantive disputes with Marxists, pluralists and participatory democrats. Beyond that in this new introduction I wish to indicate in which directions elite studies have moved and where students of politics might fruitfully extend the approach.

There are broadly two ways in which elites have interested political scientists. One is the examination of the gender, social background, education, career paths and political orientations of those persons who attain the leading positions in a range of activities that have a major bearing on societies. This approach is as much concerned with illustrating and examining the patterns of opportunities in a society as with political action. It typically examines how far elites are socially or educationally representative or, more commonly, unrepresentative of the population at large. A second approach aims to establish to what extent the members of an elite act as an elite. It asks how far the leading figures in business, unions, the media etc. have shared objectives or ideologies, coordinate their actions, control their own social reproduction. As was discussed in Chapter Two, James Meisel termed this combination of group consciousness, coherence and conspiracy the 'three Cs'. I would not now wish to describe the 'three Cs' as integral to the concept of an elite but would still wish to argue, in the manner of Meisel but in a slightly weaker form, that the study of elite action involves assessing how far the actors do display these attributes. This requires exploration of the nature and extent of networks between elite members, of internal cooperation or rivalry and of the capacity of leaders to determine the processes of recruitment to the ranks of the elite. This agenda applies whether what is being investigated is the elite of a particular sector, such as business or unions, or of a sub-sector, such as the banking business or a particular union, or is an alleged alliance of elites or even the more grandiose claim that an entire society is governed by a single controlling elite. The entire elite of a country the size of Britain might well fit into a top soccer stadium but this is not in itself evidence that the members will share common interests and values.

A recurrent problem in elite studies is the clear definition of the boundaries of the supposed elite. There must be a means of identifying who is included and whom excluded. To the degree also that, in the context of an elite approach to politics, history is an account of elite continuity, transformation and replacement there need to be criteria by which one may determine if, when and how one elite has sustained itself or has given way to another. Failure to address these issues with sufficient clarity was, it was argued in Chapter Two, a major flaw in the work of the 'classical elitists'. There has been major subsequent work, historical, conceptual and methodological, on these founding figures of elite political science which should now be consulted.[1] Those political scientists who most explicitly identify themselves as working within the classical elitist tradition have sought to confront the difficulties detected within the work of the founding fathers.[2] These modern methodological elitists have attempted to reverse what they have perceived as a preference common to Marxists, pluralists and behaviourists alike for bottom-up explanations of politics that look for ultimate determining factors amongst economic or social forces. Instead they offer top-down explanations in which elites play major independent roles in effecting political change. On these views the significance of elites arises from their degree of relative autonomy from non-elite forces (from the 'mass' in classical elite terminology). Elites are, relatively, able to choose how to act. They possess the flexibility to set the political agenda to which non-elites respond. Whilst not as unconstrained by social forces as sometimes supposed by the originators of classical elitism, elites are still regarded as having considerable resources to circumvent limitations on their freedom of action, even in apparently democratic systems. These resources include many that were identified by the classical elitists – control of recruitment to elite positions, the generation of an ideological consensus and its wider transmission in society through education and socialisation.[3]

The top-down approach of the modern elitists means that their focus is upon the relative autonomy of high politics. Politics is a sphere of elite consolidation, elite consensus or elite competition. To avoid the standard charge against elitist political science that in the final resort it merely asserts the banal truth that fewer govern than are governed, each element in any assertion of elite governance has to be more sharply defined than it frequently was by the classical founders. In many respects the crucial issue is how 'relative' is the 'relative autonomy' attributed to elites. How clearly can the values and policy priorities of an elite be distinguished from those of non-elites? It was a central complaint of Robert Dahl against elitist political science that it failed to define the scope of putative elites and, consequently, to support the contention that elites were highly autonomous and largely impervious to external pressures (see Chapter Five below). The extent to which elites are responsive to non-elite influence is clearly a central issue for any account of democracy, yet the evaluation of such responsiveness is generally impressionist and has proved difficult to measure with any exactitude.[4] In response recent exponents of the approach have sought to moderate the more extreme positions of the founders. Nordlinger has distinguished between types of elite autonomy and 'autonomy-enhancing capacities' with different implications for democratic accountability.[5] Higley and his colleagues have attempted to classify elites in terms of the extent and nature of their unity or disunity. Where an elite is internally disunited or where its members are united by a consensus on procedures but compete over substantive policy, appeals for support may be made to non-elite forces, thereby qualifying the degree to which such elites exercise autonomy.[6] Nevertheless, with these qualifications, Dogan and Higley contend that the "composition and functioning of political elites is ...the most important determinant of the type of regime that exists in a country".[7]

A major context in which elitist political science has been particularly active has been the study of transitions from authoritarian to competitive regimes that were such striking features of the political world in the 1980s and 1990s.[8] The core message of elitism is that these transformations are not to be interpreted as primarily the outcome of long-term economic or social changes. Nor are they the product of mass pressures from below. The explanation is, rather, to be found in the role of elites converging in order to negotiate understandings amongst themselves to enable violent struggles for power to be replaced by regulated elite competition. In moments of crisis elites are said to have particular room for manoeuvre and are able to take initiatives that can shape political history.

Challenges to such interpretations of transitions are often reminiscent of long-standing criticisms of elitism and turn ultimately on the claim of elite autonomy. Class-based analyses argue that elite theory ignores the extent to which elites are themselves embedded in class alignments.[9] Other bottom-up approaches have contended that the elitists greatly underestimate the roles played by mass publics in periods of political transformations and, indeed, the dependence of elites upon mass support.[10] Pluralists might similarly suggest that emergent forces of civil society played a major part in promoting and sustaining the conditions for the passage from authoritarianism to competitive democracy. A standard response to these objections within the elitist tradition since Mosca has been to claim that classes, mass publics and civil forces are rarely able to act in a spontaneous manner but are usually themselves led by emerging counter-elites or even mobilised by sections of existing elites.[11] At its most extreme this view seems to imply that all significant political action is elite-led. It is a position that can be saved from the dangers of banality or unfalsifiability only by the most careful definition of the boundaries, scope and autonomy of the elites in question.

The terms 'elite' and 'elitism' have long carried normative, ideological and sociological connotations which, as the text sought to explain, have bedevilled debates. 'Elite' has taken on commendatory tones from its connection with the elect or the best and negative associations from its implications of exclusivity at

variance with an era of egalitarian sentiment. Similarly 'elitism' has been defended as a belief in the promotion of excellence and condemned as meaning the promotion of exclusivity and privilege. The ambiguity seems particularly pronounced
in discussions of education where institutions may be praised for aiming to educate an elite and condemned for allegedly operating practices of social exclusion.
My casual impression is that 'elitism' in particular has over the last thirty years
entered more frequently into common and journalistic parlance.[12] It is used pejo-
ratively to refer to the practices of elite social reproduction that have been a central topic of elite political science since the beginning. Within political science and
sociology the study of elite reproduction has displayed an increased appreciation
of what may be called 'institutional elitism', in parallel with terms such as 'institutional racism' or 'institutional patriarchalism'. Elites may maintain their status
through procedures that systematically benefit them and disadvantage others,
without the elite members necessarily being conscious of this bias. The recognition of the importance of structural bias to understanding elite domination largely
grew out of the debates over the analysis of power sparked by the criticisms of
Dahl's decisional methodology by Bachrach and Baratz (see Chapter Five below)
and further refined in the classic work of Steven Lukes.[13] The analysis of overt
decisions might not only miss the ways in which power-holders manipulate agendas but, still more fundamentally, fail to appreciate that the very processes of
decision-making may be biased in ways not appreciated by any of the actors
involved. In part this was recognised by Pareto, Mosca and others in the elitist tradition (as well as by Marx to whom they responded) when they suggested that the
peak of elite power occurred when its ideology had gained such an hegemony in
society that neither elite nor mass was truly conscious of its existence or its bias
(Chapter Two below). The more recent analyses have, however, been rather more
concerned with structures than ideologies, although the two are interconnected.
Elites in an institution may follow long-established routines that advantage those
in office and discriminate against outsiders – women, the disabled, ethnic minorities.[14] For example, recruitment procedures which might appear open and impartial might disadvantage those who have not, by virtue of social background and
education, been in a position to obtain the requisite qualifications. The bias in such
cases may be systemic but may, nevertheless, be reversible as a result of efforts to
raise the consciousness of bias. In the case of recruitment procedures it may be
that the qualifications demanded are not as appropriate as had long been assumed
(for example, with changes to access, tasks may be shown to be performable by
the physically disadvantaged). In other cases the structural problems may be more
deeply rooted and lie outside the particular elite's immediate capacity to modify –
where, for example, fundamental changes in educational opportunities are
required before those currently disadvantaged can be in a position to achieve gen-
uinely appropriate qualifications. Any analysis of the nature of 'institutional elitism' and of the possibilities of change requires an understanding of the highly
complex relation between agency and structure – of how far those who play roles
in an established institution, whose life is given shape by the institution and who

may be the beneficiaries of it, are able to remake the structure.[15]

Chapter Three looked briefly at a number of spheres of elite activity, such as business, finance, bureaucracy and education. The objective was to illustrate the considerations that might be brought to bear in assessing the presence, nature and extent of elite domination in each arena. In that respect the text might be allowed to stand. The empirical examples discussed, however, are inevitably much changed. Taking only the instances drawn from the United Kingdom, much would need to be revised if embarking on this project at the beginning of the twenty-first century. The internal politics of the UK and its external position have undergone major changes, requiring reassessment of some of the fundamental features of British government.[16] These changes themselves offer lessons to elite analysis in that they provide evidence of the ways in which the balance of influence between strategic elites can shift markedly over a relatively short period.

The status of business and financial elites in Britain illustrates these changes and the problems of interpretation that arise. Over the last forty years Britain's domestic manufacturing sector, particularly in heavy manufactures, has shrunk markedly. Accordingly a number of very large and well-known enterprises in the 1960s have declined or even disappeared. The 1980s demonstrated that large businesses were far more vulnerable to financial takeover and merger than many had previously supposed. New service industries, often demanding different leadership profiles, have arisen. A league table of business leaders would show some major changes of position and many relegations and promotions. The phenomena of managerial buyouts and managerial share options would, moreover, seem to blur certain of the distinctions between management and capital sometimes drawn in the literature on the so-called managerial revolution. On the other side the interconnecting directorships between large firms remain widespread and subject to the same divergent interpretations as evidence of a cohesive business elite who 'run' British business or of a weaker procedural consensus beneath the surface of ruthless economic competition. The financial world of the City of London has similarly been transformed. The informal self-regulation with its social and linguistic conventions has given way to much more formal supervision. Many of the old partnerships, still with strong family connections in the 1960s, have been absorbed into major international financial conglomerates. Barings, allegedly at the centre of the supposed 'Establishment' in the 1950s, has famously and spectacularly disappeared. It is, of course, still possible to speak of the business elite or the financial elite but the landscape of both differs from what it was thirty or forty years ago.[17]

The civil service must remain on any list of strategic elites in the UK but here too the style of elite analysis would now need to be adapted to encompass changes. Up to the 1980s a hierarchical model derived from Weber's concept of bureaucracy could serve as a basis for studying recruitment, leadership and influence amongst top civil servants. Since that time, however, the structure and powers of the executive have been much altered. Privatisation has, first, removed areas of provision from the direct control of central government, including such services as public housing, telecommunications or energy supplies that had long been considered basic responsibilities. Secondly, there has been a shift in the relationship between policy advice and service delivery by the creation of a host of executive agencies led by chief executives subject to a variety of often complicated lines of public accountability. Arising from this, recruitment to many of these managerial positions has been by competition open to outsiders. The effect has been a fragmentation of the service, with policy advice and service implementation involving a wide range of governmental, independent and privatised agencies and their leaderships, many connected to wider policy networks. Political scientists attempting to describe the executive elite in the UK now face the daunting task of identifying its many manifestations and assessing their relative scope and power.[18] Elite studies have, for example, to integrate the relevant findings from the analyses of policy communities. The standard questions about elite recruitment, autonomy and scope remain but the method of analysis must now be more multi-dimensional than seemed requisite in the 1960s in order to cope with the greater complexity that has led to a preference for employing the broader term 'governance' to the implicitly specific 'government' in describing the UK's political arrangements.

The last three decades have witnessed an ebb and flow in the influence of strategic elites in Britain. The 1980s were a period of substantial reverses for trades unions with the decline of many strongly unionised industrial sectors and restrictions imposed by industrial relations legislation. The influence of manufacturing industry elites was diminished. Many professional elites – lawyers, university teachers, medical doctors – have been subject to unprecedented state regulation, with some loss of their autonomy. On the other side in an era when journalists are sometimes accused of making the news rather than reporting it, media elites would now require the attention they did not receive in the original text – not merely an examination of owners and controllers but of the background, orientations and influence of journalists and commentators. One lesson for elitist political science may be that it is necessary to avoid any in-built tendency in the approach to over-estimate the self-perpetuating capacities of elites or to neglect external social, economic and political dynamics that can result in challenges to the autonomy and relative standing of elites. A second, perhaps surprising, lesson is that, to the extent that many of the challenges to well-established elites in the 1980s were the product of the Thatcher government's antipathy to corporatism, students ignore the capacity of the elected party political elite at their peril.[19]

This last lesson would be welcome to the defenders of Schumpeter's conception of democracy as competition between political leaderships, discussed in Chapter Six on elites and democratic theory. There has continued to be a major 'realist' strain in democratic theorising that regards elite competition as one of the defining characteristics of modern democracy. The most developed exposition of the Schumpeterian model is Sartori's *Theory of Democracy Revisited* of 1987 (itself an expansion of the theme of his 1962 book discussed in Chapter Six).[20] On this view political leaderships do not merely aggregate interests so as to present rival packages of policies to the electorate. They are also expected to initiate poli-cies and actively to set agendas to which the voters respond. For this the political elites require a certain autonomy from the electorate whose role is not to govern but to select between those who compete for the authority to govern.[21] Democracy is the by-product of leadership competition. Although this is a top-down concep-tion of democracy, the final verdict lies with the electorate and for this reason vot-ers should seek to possess and cultivate political judgment. Nevertheless Sartori does not look to active popular participation in decision-making. The health of a democracy owes more to the qualities of political understanding and responsibil-ities of the competing leaderships.

Despite Robert Dahl's authorship of one of the most incisive critiques of the methodology of elitist political science in his article 'A Critique of the Ruling Elite Model', his own work has been regularly regarded as descending from the elite approach (see Chapters Five and Six). The explanation of this apparent par-adox partly lies in the form of Dahl's analysis of actually existing democracies or 'polyarchies'. He arranges polyarchies along two dimensions – liberalisation and inclusion.[22] Liberalisation refers to the emergence and presence of political con-testation, primarily between a plurality of political leaderships. Inclusion refers to the right to participate in elections and office, rather than to any specified level of active citizen involvement. It is Dahl's emphasis, in his criteria for polyarchy, on the procedures for leadership competition and on the responsiveness of leaders to electorates rather than on high levels of activism that may have led to his being aligned with democratic elitism. Moreover Dahl retained a degree of realist scep-ticism concerning expectations of widespread activism or intense communitarian-ism in the setting of liberal, pluralist societies. Nevertheless some of his later work (and certain of his very early writings) reveal a theorist far more sympathetic than his critics in the 1960s and 1970s had supposed to reforming democratic institu-tions to enable deeper citizen participation in economic and political affairs.[23]

A different perspective on the role of elites in democracy has been provided since the 1970s by the work of Arend Lijphart. His is not, however, an approach that owes anything to the classical elitist tradition. Lijphart drew attention to an alternative type of democracy to the majoritarian system familiar from the British and American tradition. In certain plural societies deeply divided on religious, lin-guistic or ethnic grounds democratic processes had arisen in which each of the main distinct segments had gained proportional representation in the national assembly, in cabinet government or in the distribution of major executive offices. Power-sharing and consensus building are essential to such polities in contrast to majoritarian systems where the winner takes all. Lijphart's term was 'consocia-tional democracy'.[24] Elites play a particular and crucial role in consociationalism. The system can only be sustained through cooperation between the segmental leaders despite the sharp differences between them. For this the elites need both to hold on to their own community constituencies and have sufficient authority from them to reach understandings and compromises or 'accommodations' with the other leaders. Elite autonomy is thus an overt feature of this style of democracy, in terms of the autonomy of each elite from the others and the freedom of action vouchsafed to them by their own followers.

Not only did Lijphart claim, sometimes controversially, to identify a significant number of countries with consociational features but, particularly in *Democracy in Plural Societies*, he advocated political engineering to establish power-sharing systems particularly in deeply divided third-world countries where, he held, they would have a much better chance of survival than majoritarian arrangements. One consequence would seem to be that the path to democracy in such countries lay first in developing autonomous elites who would in turn learn, in their own and their followers' interests, the need to cultivate the political virtues of accommodation rather than seeking to change the culture from below. Lijphart's conception of consociational or consensus democracy has been highly influential but empirically and normatively has also been subject to strong criticism. It assumes a degree of elite control of the segments and corresponding democratic self-constraint on the part of non-elites, at variance with strong participatory visions of democracy. The theory may also place excessive reliance on elite acquisition of the virtues of consensus and accommodation. It can also be true of segmental elites that their own status and interest is derived from their community and can be enhanced in the eyes of their constituency and of the wider society through pursuit of political strategies that emphasise and exploit difference and group privileges. The theory is predicated on the representation of communities rather than individuals and has perhaps appealed to those sympathetic to identity politics rather than to traditional egalitarian democrats.[25]

The other side of the coin to elite studies has been the study of citizen participation. Normative theorists have continued to argue that academic and journalistic treatments of democratic politics as if it was chiefly the province of competition between political, economic and social elites discourage popular participation much beyond involvement in the electoral process. This can also be interpreted as a potential consequence of theories of political liberalism which seek to constrain the realm of populist politics by constitutional protection of a range of rights, taking disputes about them off the political agenda, with consequent limitations on government action.[26] According to Benjamin Barber, who offers one of the most developed versions of radical participatory democracy, when politics is seen as a restricted arena populated by elites citizens become alienated and distrustful. They feel apathetic because they feel powerless. The alternative is a participatory culture where there are virtually no gags on debate or limits on the agenda and where a strong citizen bond is created through political action.[27]

Despite the initial euphoria occasioned by the transition from authoritarianism to democracy in Latin America and eastern Europe, the close of the twentieth century saw a growing concern in the established liberal democracies over an alleged crisis of citizenship, with a perceived decline in political interest and in participation even in such defining activities as general elections. Lying behind this loss of faith in democracy is said to be an impoverishment in personal social networks or 'social capital' and trust that underpinned past political engagement.[28] The issue has engaged the political elites themselves. In Britain an official report led to the unprecedented introduction of compulsory courses on citizenship in British schools. Permeating the report is a commitment to the creation of a nation of informed, enabled citizens in contrast to mere subjects of a remote, implicitly elite-dominated, state.[29] It is not certain, however, that an education in active citizenship will overcome distrust and alienation. Unless, radical critics would argue, it is accompanied by changes in the limited structures of political opportunity in liberal, representative, 'elitist' democracy the new generation educated in citizenship may merely meet with frustration rather than feel enabled.

Neo-Schumpeterian democrats might still be inclined to dismiss talk of crisis. So long as there is sufficient electoral involvement to effect or threaten an alternation of political leaderships liberal democracy is, on this view, relatively secure. Moreover the importance attached to the capacity for leadership in the complex world of modern government lends more than an iota of truth to the claims of classical elitists that democrats both need and desire strong direction in spite of their protestations. On the other side there have been significant innovations in democratic processes. The most remarkable evidence is the extent to which countries around the world have, since the 1990s, begun to adopt in their governmental arrangements a repertoire of procedures which not long before were the almost utopian proposals of radical democrats. Countries, such as Britain, which were previously antipathetic to the use of the referendum have employed them more frequently. Theorists of 'deliberative democracy' have proposed institutions which have been turned into practical experiments in several countries, such as citizen juries, in which citizens can examine policy options, cross-examine expert witnesses and debate in an informed manner, thereby, it is claimed, gaining a practical training in the modes of public reasoning.[30] It appears that the ambivalence over the roles of elites and citizens in modern democracy remains, whilst taking on new forms.

NOTES

1   See for example N. Bobbio, *On Mosca and Pareto*, Geneva, Droz, 1972; E. Albertoni, *Mosca and the Theory of Elitism*, Oxford, Blackwell, 1987; R. Bellamy, *Modern Italian Social Theory: Ideology and Politics from Pareto to the Present*, Cambridge, Polity, 1987; R. Bellamy, 'The advent of the masses and the making of the modern theory of democracy', in R. Bellamy and T. Ball, (eds), *The Cambridge History of Twentieth-Century Political Thought*, Cambridge, Cambridge University Press, 2003, pp. 70–103; J. Femia, *The Machiavellian Legacy: Essays in Italian Political Thought*, Basingstoke, Macmillan, 1998.

2   In particular see the work of G. Lowell Field, John Higley and their associates: for example, G. Lowell Field and J. Higley, *Elitism*, London, Routledge and Kegan Paul, 1980; J. Higley and R. Gunther, (eds), *Elites and Democratic Consolidation in Latin America and Southern Europe*, Cambridge, Cambridge University Press, 1992; M. Dogan and J. Higley, (eds),

Elites, Crises, and the Origins of Regimes, Lanham, Rowman and Littlefield, 1998; J. Higley and M. Burton, 'Elite Settlements and the Taming of Politics', *Government and Opposition*, 1998, Vol. 33, pp. 98–115; J. Higley and G. Lengyel, (eds), *Elites after State Socialism: Theories and analyses*, Lanham, Rowman and Littlefield, 2000; also within this tradition are E. A. Nordlinger, *On the Autonomy of the Democratic State*, Cambridge, Mass., Harvard University Press, 1981; E. Etzioni-Halevy, *The Elite Connection: Problems and Potential of Western Democracy*, Cambridge, Polity, 1993. Theoretical and empirical contributions to elite studies are collected in J. Scott, (ed.), *The Sociology of Elites*, 3 vols., Aldershot, Elgar, 1990.

3   An excellent review of the techniques available to political elites is provided by R. Putnam, *The Comparative Study of Political Elites*, Englewood Cliffs, N.J., Prentice-Hall, 1976. On elite education and social reproduction see P. Bourdieu, *The State Nobility: Elite Schools in the Field of Power*, transl. L.C. Clough, Cambridge, Polity Press, 1996.

4   Attempts at measurement at local community level include S. Verba, N. Nie and J-O. Kim, *Participation and Political Equality: A Seven-Nation Comparison*, Cambridge, Cambridge University Press, 1978, pp. 301–9; G. Parry, G. Moyser and N. Day, *Political Participation and Democracy in Britain*, Cambridge, Cambridge University Press, 1992, pp. 348–88.

5   Nordlinger, *On the Autonomy of the Democratic State*, pp. 27–41 and *passim*.

6   Field and Higley, *Elitism*, pp. 35–43; M. Dogan and J. Higley, 'Elites, Crises, and Regimes in Comparative Analysis' in Dogan and Higley (eds), *Elites, Crises, and the Origins of Regimes*, pp. 3–27.

7   Dogan and Higley, 'Elites, Crises, and Regimes in Comparative Analysis', p. 20.

8   For example D. Lane, *Elites and Political Power in the USSR*, Aldershot, Elgar, 1988; T. Rigby, *Political Elites in the USSR*, Aldershot, Elgar, 1990; G. Gill (ed.), *Elites and Leadership in Russian Politics*, Basingstoke, Macmillan, 1998; see also footnote 2.

9   P. Cammack, 'A Critical Assessment of the New Elite Paradigm', *American Sociological Review*, 1990, Vol. 55, pp. 415–20.

10 See A. Knight, 'Historical and Theoretical Considerations', in Dogan and Higley, (eds), *Elites, Crises, and the Origins of Regimes*, pp. 29–45.

11 Dogan and Higley, 'Elites, Crises, and Regimes in Comparative Analysis', pp. 24–5; compare G. Mosca, *The Ruling Class*, (ed. Livingston), New York, McGraw-Hill, 1939, Ch. IV, para. 6, pp. 6–7.

12 See, for example, 'The New British Elite', *The Times*, T2, 5–8 January 2004.

13 S. Lukes, *Power: A Radical View*, London, Macmillan, 1974; see also M. Crenson, *The Un-Politics of Air Pollution: A Study of Non-Decisionmaking in the Cities*, Baltimore, The Johns Hopkins Press, 1971; J. Gaventa, *Power and Powerlessness: Quiescence and Rebellion in an Appalachian Valley*, Oxford, Oxford University Press, 1980; P. Morriss, *Power: A Philosophical Analysis*, Manchester, Manchester University Press, 1987.

14 G. Parry and P. Morriss, 'When is a Decision not a Decision?' in I. Crewe (ed.) *British Political Sociology Yearbook: Vol. 1, Elites in Western Democracy*, London, Croom Helm, 1974, pp. 317–36.

15 On structure and agency see, for example, P. Bourdieu, *Outline of a Theory of Practice*, Cambridge, Cambridge University Press, 1977; A. Giddens, *The Constitution of Society: Outline of the Theory of Structuration*, Cambridge, Polity, 1984. Also the pioneering and

neglected study, D. Emmet, *Rules, Roles and Relations*, London, Macmillan, 1966.

16 See essays in I. Holliday, A. Gamble and G. Parry (eds), *Fundamentals in British Politics*, Basingstoke, Macmillan, 1999. For studies of the configuration of British elites since the 1970s see P. Stanworth and A. Giddens (eds), *Elites and Power in British Society*, Cambridge, Cambridge University Press, 1974; J. Scott, *Who Rules Britain?*, Cambridge, Polity, 1991.

17 On the changes in British financial markets see M. Moran, *The Politics of the Financial Services Revolution*, Basingstoke, Macmillan, 1991.

18 See D. Marsh and R. Rhodes, (eds), *Policy Networks in British Government*, Oxford, Oxford University Press, 1992; K. Theakston, *The Civil Service since 1945*, Oxford, Blackwell, 1995; P. Barberis (ed.), *The Civil Service in an Era of Change*, Dartmouth, 1997; M. Smith, *The Core Executive in Britain*, Basingstoke, Macmillan, 1999. On networks see D. Knoke, *Political Networks: The Structural Perspective*, Cambridge, Cambridge University Press, 1990.

19 On unions see D. Marsh, *The New Politics of British Trade Unionism*, Basingstoke, Macmillan, 1992; J. McIlroy, *Trade Unions in Britain Today*, Second edition, Manchester, Manchester University Press, 1995; on business: W. Grant, *Business and Politics in Britain*, Basingstoke, Macmillan, 1993; J. Scott and C. Griff, *Directors of Industry: The British corporate network, 1904–76*, Cambridge, Polity, 1984; J. Scott, *Capitalist Property and Financial Power: A comparative study of Britain, the United States and Japan*, Brighton, Wheatsheaf, 1986; J. Scott, *Corporate Business and Capitalist Classes*, Oxford, Oxford University Press, 1997; on media: J. Street, *Mass Media, Politics and Democracy*, Basingstoke, Palgrave, 2001.

20 G. Sartori, *The Theory of Democracy Revisited*, Chatham, NJ, Chatham House, 1987. See also W. Riker, *Liberalism Against Populism: A Confrontation Between the Theory of Democracy and the Theory of Social Choice*, San Francisco, Freeman, 1982.

21 For further explanations and defences of elite autonomy in representative democracy see E. Nordlinger, *On the Autonomy of the Democratic State*, pp. 203–19; B. Manin, *The Principles of Representative Government*, Cambridge, Cambridge University Press, 1997, pp. 211–38.

22 R. Dahl, *Polyarchy: Participation and Opposition*, New Haven, Yale University Press, 1971.

23 R. Dahl, *A Preface to Economic Democracy*, Cambridge, Polity, 1985; *Democracy and its Critics*, New Haven, Yale University Press, 1989; *Towards Democracy: A Journey*, Berkeley, Cal., Institute of Governmental Studies Press, University of California, 1997.

24 A. Lijphart, *Democracy in Plural Societies: A Comparative Exploration*, New Haven, Yale University Press, 1977. In later works the terminology and some aspects of the analyses change. See *Democracies: Patterns of Majoritarian and Consensus Government in Twenty-One Countries*, New Haven, Yale University Press, 1984; *Patterns of Democracy: Government Forms and Performance in Thirty-Six Countries*, New Haven, Yale University Press, 1999.

25 See, for example, W. Kymlicka (ed.), *The Rights of Minority Cultures*, Oxford, Oxford University Press, 1995; B. Barry, *Culture and Equality: An Egalitarian Critique of Multiculturalism*, Cambridge, Polity, 2001. Also B. Barry, 'Political Accommodation and Consociational Democracy', *British Journal of Political Science*, 1975, Vol. 5, pp. 477–505.

26 S. Holmes, 'Gag Rules or the Politics of Omission', in J. Elster and R. Slagstad (eds),

Constitutionalism and Democracy, Cambridge, Cambridge University Press, 1988, pp.19–58; J. Rawls, *Political Liberalism*, New York, Columbia University Press, 1993.

27 B. Barber, *Strong Democracy: Participatory Politics for a New Age*, Berkeley, University of California Press, 1984.

28 On the issue of declining citizenship see P. Norris (ed.), *Critical Citizens: Global Support for Democratic Government*, Oxford, Oxford University Press, 1999; R. Putnam, *Bowling Alone: The Collapse and Revival of American Community*, New York, Simon and Schuster, 2000; on political participation in Britain over this period see G. Parry, G. Moyser and N. Day, *Political Participation and Democracy in Britain* and publications from the ESRC Democracy and Participation Programme, e.g., C. Pattie, P. Seyd and P. Whiteley, 'Citizenship and Civic Engagement: Attitudes and Behaviour in Britain', *Political Studies*, 2003, Vol. 51, pp. 443–68.

29 Advisory Group on Citizenship, *Education for citizenship and the teaching of democracy in schools* (the 'Crick Report'), London, Qualifications and Curriculum Authority, 1998; B. Crick, *Essays on Citizenship*, London, Continuum, 2000; A. Lockyer, B. Crick and J. Annette, (eds) *Education for Democratic Citizenship: Issues of Theory and Practice*, Aldershot, Ashgate, 2003.

30 See for example J. Fishkin, *Democracy and Deliberation: New Directions for Democratic Reform*, New Haven, Yale University Press, 1991; A. Gutmann and D. Thompson, *Democracy and Disagreement*, Cambridge, Mass., Harvard University Press, 1996; J. Elster (ed.), *Deliberative Democracy*, Cambridge, Cambridge University Press, 1998; J. Dryzek, *Deliberative Democracy and Beyond: Liberals, Critics, Contestations*, Oxford, Oxford University Press, 2000.

political | introduction
elites |

Ever since the issue of the political role of elites – small minorities who appear to play an exceptionally influential part in political and social affairs – was first explicitly raised with relation to liberal societies in the closing decades of the nineteenth century, it has remained a central concern of political science, sociology, and political and social thought. For some, elites are the 'decision-makers' of the society whose power is not subject to control by any other body in the society. For others, elites are the sole source of values in the society or constitute the integrating force in the community without which it may fall apart. Elites have been regarded as the chief threat to the survival of democracy. Their existence has been taken to be the very denial of democracy. Elites which have exceptional access to 'key positions' in the society, or which appear to wield control over crucial policies disproportionate to their numbers can understandably seem to be living contradictions of the notion of 'government by the people'. Despite this, other writers have seen elites as the bulwarks of democracy, protecting it from the dangers of totalitarianism.

It is impossible therefore to begin a study of the use of the elite concept in political science and political thought with a definition of 'elite'. Instead, one must trace the usage of the word, and related terms such as 'power elite', 'social elite', 'oligarchy', 'ruling class' in the literature of the subject. One must make clear the distinctions between these terms and show how such contradictory views of elites can have been held.

The present study will be concerned with 'elites in politics'. Hence its subject will not be merely 'politicians' to whom the term 'political elite' is sometimes confined. It will look at the many minority groups, each with its inner group of leaders, which attempt to exert some influence, legitimate or otherwise, over the allocation of values in a society. Business interests, unions, the military, the bureaucrats are to be regarded as 'political elites' for the present purpose.

Being concerned with elites as a concept of political science and of modern political and social theory, this study will not discuss any of the grand, openly prescriptive theories of elites produced in the past, such as Plato's, in which an elite is proposed as the one guarantee of political 'truth' or 'virtue' or 'success' or mere 'stability', although echoes of such a view may be heard when contemporary democratic theory is discussed in the final chapter. Nor should the reader expect any 'inside dope'. This is not, or should not be, the object of elite studies, however much it enlivens the narrative, particularly in the studies of community power.

The object of elite studies is, rather, to examine the structure of power in communities, to see whether it is in the hands of a cohesive, self-conscious minority, to test whether this is an inevitable or a merely contingent development, and in doing so to illuminate the question of the nature of 'power'. A prime aim of this book, then, is to provide a critical review of recent work in political science which has attempted to test the hypothesis that in all communities influence is concentrated in the hands of a single cohesive elite, or, which is not the same thing, of a very small minority of the population. Such tests have most often been in the form of studies of local communities, and the best known of such works will be looked at in some detail.

Empirical studies which do not begin with some conceptual framework or some hypothesis to test are foredoomed to failure, if they are indeed possible at all. This review will begin, therefore, by outlining the chief rival hypotheses – on the one hand that elite rule is inevitable and on the other, that power in societies is widely distributed between a variety of rival groups which include or represent the bulk of the population. It will look at the context in which these hypotheses emerged: the political and social circumstances, as well as the state of political studies. Finally, it will trace the way in which empirical political science has raised in a new form some fundamental problems of democratic theory.

Political institutions, political behaviour, political power and political ideology all find a place in the controversies surrounding elites. Elitists have forced political philosophers to reconsider the status of many of the values commonly associated with democracy, such as equality and liberty, and consequently have impelled a revision of democratic theory. Even the opponents of the theory of elitism have been unable to ignore its conclusions.

chapter | the context of elite theorising
one |

The study of elites was established as part of political science in the late nine-teenth and early twentieth centuries largely as a result of the work of two Italian sociologists, Vilfredo Pareto (1848–1923) and Gaetano Mosca (1858–1941). Political theory always reflects on political practice and in many ways the politi-cal circumstances of the time favoured attempts to theorise about the nature of control and the role of leadership in society. The state appeared to be extending its influence into areas of society with which for a long time previously it had shown little concern. Governments were legislating on such matters as the limitation of hours of work, the regulation of working conditions and the provision of pensions and other rudiments of the welfare state.

A celebrated series of lectures by A. V. Dicey argued that even in England the years since 1870 had witnessed a revolutionary change, whereby legislative col-lectivism had displaced individualistic liberalism as the principle behind govern-ment action.[1] In order to administer these measures the executive branches of gov-ernment had to be extended and made more efficient. The trend towards a stronger executive had been continuing intermittently since the seventeenth century and there were clear indications by the late nineteenth century that this process was being furthered rather than arrested in the more democratic states. The civil serv-ice was being organised on more bureaucratic lines. The establishment of modern bureaucracy was hailed by many as part of a progress towards a more open soci-ety and even a step towards the democratisation of government. Bureacracy offered a 'career open to the talents' and its establishment was a major aim of many nineteenth century liberals. In principle, entry into government service was now open to any man of talent and was not dependent on influence or patronage.

Bureaucratic administrations also appeared to provide constraints on the free use of governmental power. Bureaucracy operates according to deliberately con-structed rules. These rules lay down a hierarchy of administrative offices and the scope and responsibility of each. The holder of any office can act authoritatively only so long as he carries out the duties laid down in the rules. Neither the gov-ernment nor the individual office holder is owner of the means of administration, the bureaucracy being itself part of the legal order which constitutes the state. The effect of this system was to require that governmental orders were issued in the form of general rules which could be administered and applied in an impersonal and impartial manner. The rule might still, of course, be inappropriate or evil, but its very character as a rule of conduct excluded sheer arbitrariness. Although the government might be the possessor of absolute legislative authority, it committed itself to carrying out its laws according to known, formal procedures. Bureaucracy thus contributed to the traditional constitutionalist ideal of the 'rule of law'.

Bureaucracy, however, had another side to it which was noted in particular by Max Weber, who brilliantly traced both bureaucracy's liberalising and its dominating aspects.[2] Bureaucracy permitted a more efficient organisation of power. The clear hierarchical organisation and stipulation of responsibilities allowed commands to flow smoothly from the top – central government ministers and their chief officials – to the bottom – the local officials applying the decision 'on the ground'. The individual citizen could face the full organised strength of the state in any area of his life in which the state had decided to intervene. Bureaucracy enabled state power to be organised more efficiently than ever before in history.

This efficient organisation need not, however, be used merely to assist the legislative authority to apply its laws. The efficiency of the state bureaucracy could permit it to appropriate the decision-making and policy-forming power from the *de jure* political authority. This possibility arises from the technical expertise of the bureaucrats. The official is appointed and promoted for his technical competence and knowledge, which is enhanced in the course of official work. If an official has worked for any length of time in an executive department, such as the Department of Agriculture, he will have obtained a considerable expertise on such matters as price policies, subsidies, land use and the views of the major agricultural interest groups. Moreover, this knowledge would itself be efficiently organised. A bureaucracy operates through written documents which are filed for record and speedy reference. As a result of its long-standing concern with an issue a department may formulate a policy line of its own with which each official is indoctrinated, and which can be concerted with ease as a result of the organisational advantages of the bureaucracy and the *ésprit de corps* which such a body readily develops.

In form the political chief – the minister – is the bureaucrat's superior whose task it is to formulate the policies which the officials will carry out. In practice, however, the political superior may, as Weber suggested, be an amateur in the subject as compared with his officials. To a considerable extent he may have to rely on his officials for information which they are in a position to organise and select. He may have to fight for his policy against the concerted policy of his department; be prepared to set his lay judgement against their combined expertise. Often, although the minister will retain his formal responsibility for making policy, he may become the spokesman of his officials. The bureaucracy becomes the *de facto* policy-maker without being fully answerable to the public. In an extreme case the society is governed by a bureaucratic absolutism that treats the people as objects to be administered rather than as participating citizens and decides issues on grounds of secret administrative convenience. At best bureaucracy offers enlight-

ened paternalism, at worst careerism, routine and 'red tape'; at all times government is remote and in a strict sense irresponsible. Weber cited as such an extreme
case German politics from the period of Bismarck to the First World War, which
in turn was part of a pattern of Prussian bureaucratic government since the eighteenth century.

The study of bureaucracy thus indicated a new highly efficient potential power
behind the recognised political authority. At the very least the bureaucracy constituted a new source of political influence. Some regarded it as the real power
behind the sham power of the government.

The trend towards a stronger executive continued at the same time as the franchise in many countries in Europe was extended to much larger sections of the
community. From the 1860s onwards the general outlines of modern mass democratic politics were laid down. In principle this permitted a larger proportion of the
people to participate in determining the political affairs of their country.
'Government by the people' and 'the will of the people' seemed apt slogans to
describe the developing political situation and the aims of the reformers. As early
as 1861, however, John Stuart Mill had warned of the fallacy of identifying 'self-
government' with individual self-determination. Rule by the majority implied
merely rule by the majority amongst those elected by the majority. Liberty would
still need to be safeguarded against this ruling group. The controllers still had, if
not to be controlled, at least to be kept under close surveillance. Nevertheless Mill
believed that a mass influence in political affairs was not to be avoided and strove
rather to ensure that the majority should at least be enlightened by the participation in the Parliament of representatives of the intelligent minority of the community. This was to be attained in part by a system of fancy franchises giving extra
votes to the better educated and the more technically qualified, so as to ensure the
appearance of 'the very elite of the country' in Parliament.[3] This elite would still
be a minority in the assembly, but the intelligence of their contribution to debate
would force the majority to raise the standard of their own arguments and gradually raise the standard of political reasoning as a whole. Mill's aim was neither to
predict nor to justify elite rule, but the liberal goal of raising the level of culture
and enlightenment in a democratic society.

But it was Walter Bagehot who, in 1867, hinted in his *The English Constitution*
at the line that was to be adopted by so many writers on mass democracy. The
masses could be accommodated in the existing system only if they could be per-
suaded to accept the political direction of a minority. This the masses could be
expected to do. They would follow an idea, such as glory, empire or nation – what
Mosca was to term a 'political formula', Pareto a 'derivation' and others an 'ideology' or a 'myth'. The masses would defer to the 'theatrical show' of the 'digni-
fied part' of the constitution, would believe that the queen rules and not merely
reigns. The masses cheer the apparent rulers in the splendid leading coaches of the
procession whilst:

The real rulers are secreted in second-rate carriages; no-one cares for them or asks about them, but they are obeyed implicitly and unconsciously by reason of the splendour of those who eclipsed and preceded them.[4]

As a result of its deferential behaviour the majority "...abdicates in favour of its *elite*, and consents to obey whoever that *elite* may confide in".[5] So long as this disposition continued in the masses, the established leadership need not fear being displaced as a result of an extended franchise. The 'will of the people' thus threatened to be a myth concealing the continued rule of an uncontrolled minority.

One result of the extension of the franchise was the emergence of the mass parties. The parties sought the support of the expanded electorate, opening membership to all who possessed the vote and who were willing to subscribe to the party's aims. The more radical parties even established constitutions, which aimed at ensuring that the party's leaders stayed in line with the policies laid down by the mass conference representing the party members. In Britain Liberal Associations grew up on the model of Joseph Chamberlain's Birmingham 'Caucus' of 1867 with the object of organising the Liberal vote. A decade later Chamberlain established the National Liberal Federation, composed of delegates elected from the Liberal Associations. By this time the object had become that of coordinating and proposing policy for the Parliamentary party to act upon and even of pressuring the party to follow certain lines of action. Chamberlain saw the Federation as a "Liberal Parliament outside the imperial legislature". For a brief period from 1883 to 1884 Lord Randolph Churchill sought, undoubtedly for personal ends, to turn the National Union of Conservative Associations from being a handmaid of the party into being its elected manager. In the USA more far-reaching attempts were made from the 1880s onward to bring the parties under popular control by means of primary elections to determine the selection of candidates. At first the primaries were indirect, involving the election of delegates to a convention for the selection of candidates, but after 1903 when the first mandatory state-wide direct primary was established in Wisconsin the direct primaries rapidly displaced the convention system enabling wider participation in the selection of candidates.

Once again, then, the political system might appear to be opening up under the pressures of mass politics. But once again there were sceptics. Lord Randolph Church might affirm that "...in a struggle between a popular body and a closed corporation, the latter, I am happy to say, in these days goes to the wall".[6] But contemporary students of political parties saw things in a different light. Ostrogorski, looking at the emergence of the mass party in England at the end of the nineteenth century, concluded that the caucus would gain power over the party but would itself become the machine of a small group of men not accountable to the public.[7] Robert Michels, a disciple of Mosca and friend of Max Weber, in a celebrated study of the German Social Democrats, concluded that the tendency would be for control of parties to fall into the hands of a combination of parliamentary leaders and party bureaucrats.[8] In fact, the power of the extra-parliamentary bodies was defeated in Britain by the established parliamentary leaderships in whose hands party control has by and large remained ever since. In the USA the primary sys-

tem did not in most cases dislodge the local party leadership's control of nominations. Thus the party leaderships in the Western democracies did not succumb to
pressures from the masses, whilst in Russia Lenin was advocating the bureaucratisation of the revolutionary movement.[9]

The same process was going on in economic life. Industry was increasing in
scale and in concentration. The new trades unions, having sampled various techniques of control by direct democracy, had rapidly evolved into oligarchies operating behind a democratic facade – a development welcomed by their great historians, the Webbs, as a step towards more effective organisation.[10] It is therefore not
surprising that this new age of mass democracy should have been described
recently as the 'age of organisation'.[11] At the same time there was a growing
awareness of the role of non-rational forces in politics[12] and in particular of the
ability of propaganda to exploit these forces in the interests of rulers.

Mass politics and large scale organisation were, thus, two aspects of the new
political experience of the last years of the nineteenth and the early years of the
twentieth century. Students of politics were with one breath relating the advent of
the mass into politics – were discovering 'the crowd' – and with the next breath
were saying that power had never been more restricted to a narrow few. It is not,
in the circumstances, surprising that these students began to ask whether or not the
various leadership groups, in parliament, the parties, the bureaucracies, in industry, showed signs of being concentrated into a single elite. They aimed to enquire
about the techniques of leadership, the relations between leaders and led and what
sorts of people attained positions of leadership. Elite studies were thus coeval with
the era of modern politics and offered a way of understanding its structure, in particular the aspect that many saw as central – the relationship between leaders and
the masses.

ELITISM AS A SCIENCE AND AS IDEOLOGY

The explanations which the elitists proposed for the shape of modern politics
were, they claimed, 'scientific'. Indeed, several of the elitists saw themselves as
contributing to the establishment of a neutral, 'objective' political science, free
from any ethical contamination. Mosca opens The Ruling Class by contrasting the
successes of the natural sciences in explaining physical phenomena by subsuming
them under general laws with the failure to achieve parallel success in the social
sciences. The first chapter offers a discussion of the methods appropriate to a
political science. Pareto is similarly concerned with the methodological foundations of social science. Indeed, the analysis of elites is for Mosca and Pareto, only
one part of a much wider 'scientific' analysis of society and of the role of politics
within it. The methods suggested were not necessarily identical with those adopted by the natural sciences. In fact, both Mosca and Pareto insisted on the differences between the natural and social sciences imposed by the nature of the material studied. What they did claim for their approaches was the same objectivity as

that of natural science. This objectivity, they believed, was strikingly absent in previous thinking about politics.

Mosca argued that writers in the past had been concerned in the main to make recommendations about politics rather than discover the principles according to which political systems work. Even those past thinkers most frequently described as 'political scientists', such as Machiavelli,

> ...were less concerned with determining constant trends in human societies than with the arts by which an individual, or a class of individuals, might succeed in achieving supreme power in a given society and in thwarting the efforts of other individuals or groups to supplant them.[13]

A distinction had to be made between politics as the art of governing and politics as the science of government. Both he and Pareto interpreted even the past attempts at a social science as themselves instances of recommendations or ideologies.[14] Pareto dismissed the great sociological systems of the nineteenth century – such as those of Comte or Spencer – as merely another form of religion.[15]

In place of religion and moralising the elitists offered laws and facts. Mosca's so-called 'historical method' of political science was founded on "the study of the facts of society" and he added that "those facts can be found only in the history of the various nations".[16] Previous generations had lacked the accurate knowledge of history now available and so were unable to formulate from such knowledge the "constant facts and tendencies", the "incontrovertible truths which would not have been discovered by the ordinary observation of the plain man",[17] that constitute the propositions of science. For many, though not all, of the elitists these tendencies amounted to laws which, like the laws of physics, permitted of no exceptions. Their operation was inevitable regardless of any human efforts to counteract them. According to Michels, the law of oligarchy which he formulated on the basis of the 'facts of experience' was 'inevitable' and "an essential characteristic of all human aggregates" and "historical evolution mocks all the prophylactic measures that have been adopted for the prevention of oligarchy".[18] These laws, being accurate hypotheses as to the working of political systems, were not concerned with the morality or justice of such systems. The elitists disclaimed any intention of making any ethical comment on the phenomena they describe.

According to Michels the 'law of oligarchy', like every other sociological law, was 'beyond good and evil'[19] and it was "not the task of science to inquire whether this phenomenon is good or evil, or predominantly one or the other..."[20] Pareto declared "We do not propose to concern ourselves at all with the intrinsic 'truth' of any religion, faith, metaphysical or moral belief whatever...we refuse to discuss whether an act is just or unjust, moral or immoral..."[21] James Burnham, a self-styled follower of what he once termed the Machiavellianism of the elitists,[22] put their viewpoint well in a celebrated work:[23]

> I am not writing a *programme* of social reform, nor am I making any *moral*

judgement whatever on the subject...I am not concerned...with whether the facts indicated by this theory are 'good' or 'bad', just or unjust, desirable or undesirable – but simply with whether the theory is true or false on the basis of the evidence now at our disposal...

Because the bulk of past political thought had, the elitists believed, been mere subjective moralising on the part of its authors, it had made no contribution to the advancement of a scientific understanding of politics. Its conclusions were incapable of empirical testing. Pareto's treatment of Rousseau may serve as an instance.

So he goes prating on, and discovers, starting from the 'nature' of things, how things *must* have been, and all this without being put to the trouble of verifying his fine theories by facts, since at the outset he stated that he was setting them aside.[24]

The only interest for a social scientist in such theories is to explain their popular appeal: "Be it remembered that there are still many, many people who admire such meaningless drivel; that is why it has to be taken into account if one intends to study human society".[25] The political thought of the past was not, however, rejected in its entirety. Mosca, in particular, recognised himself as extending a tradition of empirical political science which stretched from Aristotle, through Machiavelli, Montesquieu, Saint-Simon, Marx and the evolutionary writers of his day.[26] This is not to deny that Mosca was highly critical of these writers, particularly of Aristotle and Marx. His treatment of Aristotle is characteristic. The normative framework of Aristotle's study is neglected and the philosophy of law and of justice ignored in order to concentrate on Aristotle the 'political scientist'. Mosca describes Aristotle's attempts to establish the administratively correct plan and size for cities, to formulate a theory of types of government, to discover the laws of political change. What Mosca presents is the history of political doctrines as the history of tentative efforts to establish a science of politics.

The elitists never wished to deny at least one ethical commitment though it was a commitment which they could properly regard as part of scientific enquiry. They set out to destroy the many illusions which they believed had hampered the discovery of political 'reality'. These illusions were many and various. They concerned the status of political ideals such as 'equality' or 'the rule of law', and the nature of the 'laws' of political science discovered by their predecessors. The illusions they were especially concerned with were those concerning the distribution of political power in societies. These illusions were shared by ordinary citizens, by political philosophers and political slogan writers (much the same thing to the elitists), by liberals and by socialists. In particular these illusions were fostered and promoted by the very men who professed to know better – the political historians and the political scientists. Some of these illusions had been handed down for centuries. The most notorious of these was Aristotle's classification of political constitutions, which had remained the accepted manner of classification into the nineteenth century. Aristotle had used three main criteria in his classification – the number of persons who could wield political authority in the society, their degree of wealth and whether those in authority governed in the interests of the whole community or only in their own interests. This suggested six types of constitution-kingship, aristocracy and 'polity' or 'mixed government' and their deviant forms, tyranny, oligarchy and democracy.

The only major revision of Aristotle's typology before the nineteenth century was by Montesquieu who suggested that the number of rulers was an inadequate criterion of classification. A proper classification should, instead, take into account differences in the machinery of government, in the degree of political participation and in the legitimacy of the government. Whether a government operated according to the rule of law was a more distinguishing feature for comparison than the number who participated in ruling. Thus tyrannies and oligarchies which did not recognise the rule of law constituted a common type – despotism – whereas aristocracies and democracies, which both governed according to law and by means of assemblies, constituted another common type – republics. Montesquieu concluded that there were three 'ideal types' of political system-monarchy, republic and despotism – to which any actual given political system would approximate.

Mosca led the elitists in emphatically rejecting these typologies. To compare political systems on these bases was to be misled by appearances. The various constitutions which Aristotle distinguished were mere legal 'fronts' behind which was always to be found a small ruling class who wielded the real political power in the society. One must distinguish between the *de jure* authority and the *de facto* authority or, rather, between the formal structure of political authority and the informal structure of political power. The constitution may place sovereignty in the hands of the whole people in a democracy or in the hands of the upper classes by wealth or birth in an aristocracy or in the hands of a single person in a monarchy. In every case, however, an organised minority – a political class, defining 'political' in a wide sense – took the real decisions. A king's decisions were always taken with the participation of his advisers, in an aristocracy a smaller group of activists made the policies issued in the name of all the aristocrats and in a democracy the sovereign electorate was manipulated by the politicians.

To the elitists the older typologies were merely outstanding instances of political myths propagated as political science by students of comparative politics. There were other ideas of much greater consequence. These were the ideas that were not confined to the political scientists but had been accepted by politicians and public alike as laws or truths about modern society which could then be used as guides for political action. The elitists, and Pareto in particular, argued that these accepted truths or laws were a rationalisation of either the hopes, the aspirations or the interests of those holding them or those who originated them. What had been held to be objective truth was thus revealed to be ideology. The elitists believed that one 'truth' and one 'law' in particular, needed to be exposed as ideology. The supposed 'truth' was that in mass democracies government was 'by the people'. The very intention of Mosca's *The Ruling Class* was to refute this Rousseauistic myth, as he saw it, of popular sovereignty.[27] Government in a democracy was certainly *of* the people, it might even be *for* the people, but it was never *by* the people but only by the ruling class. The supposed 'law' which required refutation was that asserted by socialists according to which a classless, egalitarian society would be the inevitable outcome of the class-conflict which had characterised all previous history. This law was a mere pious hope which deceived the lower classes in society, but at the same time significantly bolstered their confidence. As such it was no different from the many religions which had performed the same task. Pareto expressed this in his usual caustic tone. "It is, paradoxically, precisely the inequality of men which prompts them to proclaim their equality".[28] The only true law was that society would always be ruled by an elite of some sort.

It is this belief that they are exposing truths long hidden by ideology, by sentiments and by political machinations that gives the elitists the air of confidence which is characteristic of their writing. They share the mood that pervaded other areas of thought at that period and has continued to play a great part in the intellectual life of this century – the conviction that all statements to be true must be empirically verifiable, a test that would distinguish science from religion, truth from metaphysics in philosophy, and myth from reality in politics.

The objectivity of elitist writing was, however, much less than its practitioners claimed and it is, perhaps, not unfair that writers so keen to interpret the scientific theories of others as self-interested ideologies should be hoist with their own petards. Elitism was on the definitions of the elitists themselves an 'ideology' or 'formula'. It offered a defence, in rationalistic or scientific terminology, of the political interests and status of the middle class. Mosca not only showed that elite domination was inevitable even in modern democratic societies, but he also showed that the elite would be composed of the middle class. The talents and advantages of the middle class would ensure its inevitable dominance and, even if only as a by-product, his works indicated the means by which the middle class could continue to compose the elite. Mosca's later work became, in fact, a eulogistic defence of nineteenth century representative government in which the still, small voice of reason of the middle class triumphed by virtue of its control of political power in parliament, party and elections, and by virtue of the political intelligence it showed in accommodating the pressures on it from other social and economic forces. Robert Michels, following up lines hinted at by his master Mosca, predicted that leaders of the new socialist parties who were proletarians by origin would rapidly become 'bourgeoisified' once they were in positions of power. They would inevitably exchange workshop floor for office and public platform. As they were drawn into the fundamentally middle class parliamentary politics they would become as bourgeois in their way of life as their opponents in the established parties. They would undergo the process of 'assimilation' into the middle-class elite which was to be a recurrent element in elitist analysis.

Such writing could give encouragement to a class which in many countries of

Europe, including Italy – the source of so much elitist thought – had only recently gained political power at the expense of the aristocracy, but was already threatened from below by a working class quickly gaining in political consciousness
and in organised strength. The faint-hearted might think that the era of middle
class political power was over almost as soon as it had started. The elitists could
offer the middle class assurance that the trend of the times lay with it. In Italy both
Pareto and Mosca were hailed by conservatives as ideologists of the middle
class.[29] Such an assurance must have seemed all the more urgent since the working
class was already armed with an ideology, masked as a science. Marxist socialism
offered the proletariat more than hopeful slogans. It offered what appeared to be,
and was claimed to be, a science of society which explained the class relationship
within existing and all hitherto existing societies and predicted the eventual
inevitable dominance of the working class to be followed in turn by the replacement of class rule by a classless society. The comprehensive character of Marx's
social analysis was unrivalled. The status of politics and political leadership, the
role of the middle class and of representative institutions, the character of
ideology, the situation of the masses – all were within the compass of 'scientific
socialism'. It is therefore scarcely surprising that an answer to Marxism was
sought by those whose doom Marx had foretold.

MARXISM AND ELITISM

The character of elitist thinking cannot be fully understood if the impact of
Marxism on it is not appreciated. The 'classic' elitists – Pareto and Mosca – were
as much concerned to refute Marx as they were to explore an ethically neutral
political science. Later elitists, such as Burnham and to some extent, C. Wright
Mills, attempted to synthesise elements of Marx with elements from the originally antagonistic elitist position. The reply to Marx was necessarily, given the character of both Marxism and elitism, on two levels – it attacked Marxism as science
and attacked it as ideology. With Marxism, however, elitism of course shared an
inability to see itself as ideology rather than science. Pareto illuminates both the
elitist attitude to Marx and the impact of Marxism. His motivation was to demonstrate that Marx's analysis was undoubtedly false and also to explain how such, to
his mind obvious, falsehoods had gained the widespread allegiance that they had.
To achieve this Pareto developed a system which could answer point for point the
Marxist account of the economy, politics and ruling and which could reduce
Marxism's status from that of a science to that of an ideology or a religious myth.

As a consequence elitism parallels Marxism very closely in the problems discussed, although the solutions proffered by elitism are so different. Marx had
already exposed the liberal myths which surrounded the political institutions of
modern societies. To the extent that political analysts, economists and philosophers believed their accounts of political systems and the ideals they proclaimed
to have universal validity they were, Marx said, themselves victims of the 'illu-

sion of the epoch'. They were accepting as truth what was in fact part of the ideological support of the ruling class. The elitists accepted much of this argument but whilst Marx intended this exposure to be a stimulus to working class revolutionary action, the elitists gave it a middle class bent. Such myths were an inevitable part of any feasible political system and could no more be abolished than could the inequalities they justified or concealed. The inability of Marxists to recognise this inevitability was one of the elements in the theory which, for the elitists, exposed it as an ideology for the working class rather than the science of society which it claimed to be. Pareto in particular recognised that Marxists do not make this distinction between what is fact and what is value, holding as they do that a scientific theory should lead to practical action. But Pareto also placed this argument in another perspective. The scientific quality or accuracy of such theorising was irrelevant to its success in winning adherents. Marxism, like other religions, could only be understood as an elaborate rationalisation, suitable to its times, of certain basic, universal human instincts.

To Marx's account of history in terms of the conflict of economic classes the elitists oppose political interpretations. Elitists do not, with the exception of Burnham, see politics as a mere reflection of the economic class structure. For Pareto and Mosca the power structure of any society is determined by the character and abilities of its political leadership. It is political skill – or the lack of it – which determines who will rule and how power may change hands. According to Marx, by contrast, the political leader from whatsoever class he may himself be drawn, is but the 'representative' of the dominant economic class. Only where there is a balance between classes can a political elite gain any independence of action. The elitist does not deny that economic factors are important but insists that by political means an elite can control, accommodate or even counter-act economic forces. In Marx the significant social tensions are between the class which owns the prevailing means of production and hence rules the society and the ruled class or classes whose economic position impels them to organise in antagonism to the ruling class. In the elitist thesis the tension is between the dominant political elite and any rival elite which may arise to challenge for power. The mass of the population is unorganised and only becomes politically significant when it is unified by an elite. A prime effect of Marx's theory was therefore to stimulate a rival doctrine which sought to rescue politics and political leadership from the subordinate position to which he had relegated them.

The elitists thus attacked Marxism on three points. Firstly, they had the polemical intention of exposing Marx's theory as a time-bound ideology for the working class in capitalist societies rather than the science of society and the guide for action which it claimed to be. Secondly, they rejected Marx's prediction of a future classless, egalitarian society finding no justification for Marx's belief that the hierarchical structure of society was not inevitable. Thirdly, they challenged the view that economics rather than politics was the determining force in history and the bond that held societies together.

Despite the radical opposition between Marxism and elitism there have, in

more recent years, been attempts, notably by James Burnham and to some extent
by C. Wright Mills, to effect a synthesis of Marx, Mosca and Pareto. The resultant accounts attempt to place leadership in both its economic and its political context rather than emphasise unduly one rather than the other. So widespread have
such syntheses become that critics have fastened on them the title of the 'ruling
elite model' to describe a position alleged to incorporate both Marxist and elitist
elements. In any strong sense the two theories are clearly irreconcilable. If
divorced from the grand theories surrounding them, however, (and this is no easy
task) notions of class and of elite can very often be used to supplement one another and, as will be seen, important questions can be raised as to the relations
between elites and the class structure in specific social contexts. In part, this complementary use of class and elite is possible because Marxism and elitism never
quite met head on. Marx's work was basically a response to modern industrial
society; elitism was a response to modern political developments. Despite their
comprehensiveness neither was able to get both the economic and the political
into a balanced perspective.

NOTES

1   A. V. Dicey, *Law and Public Opinion in England during the Nineteenth Century*, Macmillan,
    London, 1905.
2   Weber's first analysis of bureaucracy was written between 1911 and 1913. See *From Max
    Weber* (ed. Gerth & Mills) Routledge, London, 1957, pp 196–244. Also R. Bendix, *Max
    Weber*, Heinemann, London, 1960, pp. 418 ff.
3   *Representative Government*, Blackwell, Oxford, 1946, p. 198. Mill appears to be one of the
    first to use the term 'elite' in a political context.
4   Bagehot, *The English Constitution* (ed. Crossman), Fontana, London, 1963, p.249
5   *The English Constitution*, p. 247.
6   Quoted in R. T. McKenzie, *British Political Parties*, Heinemann, London, 1955, p. 172.
7   M. Ostrogorski, *Democracy and the Organisation of Political Parties*, Macmillan, London,
    1902.
8   Michels, *Political Parties*, Free Press, Glencoe, 1915. (First published in German in 1911.)
9   Lenin, *What is to be done?*
10 S. & B. Webb, *Industrial Democracy*, Longmans, London, 1897; see also V. L. Allen, *Power
    in Trade Unions*, Longmans, London, 1954.
11 S. S. Wolin, *Politics and Vision*, Allen & Unwin, London, 1961, Ch. 10.
12 See, e.g., Graham Wallas, *Human Nature in Politics*, Constable, London, 1908.
13 Mosca, *The Ruling Class*, (ed. A. Livingston), McGraw-Hill, New York, 1939, p. 1.
14 Mosca, *The Ruling Class*, p. 6.
15 *The Mind and Society*, Harcourt Brace, New York, 1935, §6. *Sociological Writings*, ed. S. E.
    Finer, Pall Mall Press, London, 1966, p. 171. Henceforth citations will be given where pos-
    sible from *Sociological Writings* followed by the paragraph number of *The Mind and Society*

in brackets. Otherwise the paragraph number alone will be cited.

16 *The Ruling Class*, p. 41.
17 *The Ruling Class*, p. 3.
18 *Political Parties*, p. 423.
19 *Political Parties*, p. vii.
20 *Political Parties*, p. 417.
21 *Sociological Writings*, pp. 172–3 (§69).
22 J. Burnham, *The Machiavellians*, John Day, New York, 1943 (republished Gateway, Chicago, 1963).
23 *The Managerial Revolution*, Putnam, London, 1942, p. 7.
24 *Sociological Writings*, p. 212 (§821).
25 Ibid.
26 G. Mosca, *Histoire des doctrines politiques*, Payot, Paris, 1936.
27 *The Ruling Class*, p. 52.
28 *Sociological Writings*, p. 164; *Manuel d'Economie Politique*, §116, 1909.
29 See G. Prezzolini, 'L'aristocrazia dei briganti', from *Il Regno*, 1903, reprinted in *La Cultura italiana del' 900 attraverso le reviste*, Vol. I, 1960. I am indebted to Dr V. Lucchesi of the University of Oxford for this reference.

chapter two | the classical elitist thesis

The 'classic' texts of elitist thought are undoubtedly Pareto's *The Mind and Society* (*Treatise of General Sociology*), Mosca's The *Ruling Class* and Michels's *Political Parties*. To these might be added Burnham's *The Managerial Revolution* and C. Wright Mills's *The Power Elite*. These latter might have become classics if only by virtue of the controversy they have aroused in the last decades, but they also display a conscious continuity with the earlier classics both in the issues with which they are concerned and in some of their presuppositions. In particular, they are concerned, as, by and large, the earlier classics were, with examining the existence and nature of a single cohesive elite which dominates the affairs of a society. Much other recent writing on elites has, by contrast, been concerned with leadership in societies which are seen as composed of a number of elites which are potential competitors for influence in the society. This more pluralistic version of elitist thought will be discussed in the next chapter. In this chapter the general features of the 'classical' elitist thesis will be outlined, to be followed by a closer examination of the individual versions of this thesis put forward by its principal protagonists.

The core of the elitist doctrine is that there may exist in any society a minority of the population which takes the major decisions in the society. Because these decisions are of such wide scope, affecting the most general aspects of the society, they are usually regarded as *political* decisions even where the minority taking them are not 'politicians' in the usual sense of members of a government or legislative. Thus Mosca's 'political class' includes the wider circle of those who influence governmental decisions as well as those who formally 'decide' policies. According to the classical elitist thesis the minority gains its dominant position by means beyond ordinary election. Thus the elite may be powerful as a result of the revolutionary overthrow of the previously dominant group as in the case of the early Bolshevik leadershoip in the Soviet Union. The elite may owe its position to conquest – the Norman rulers of Saxon England after 1066. It may be powerful because of its monopoly of the crucial productive resources of a society such as the control of water power in oriental societies,[1] or its influence may be due to its embodying in fact or in appearance certain social or religious values widely shared in a tradition-bound society. Max Weber interpreted the status of the

Brahmins in India in this manner. But even where, as is normally the case in modern societies, the dominant minority at the very least includes some who have been elected to positions of leadership the elitists claim that electoral victory is not gained entirely by open democratic means. The appearance of democratic majority control over the minority is deceptive. The minority is in a position to manipulate the electoral process to its own ends by means of a range of measures from sheer coercion of voters, through bribery or the skilled use of propaganda to the selection of the candidates. The sovereign electorate will 'choose' its leaders from those acceptable to the elite.

In such ways the dominant minority escapes the control of the majority. The elitist thesis does not merely assert that in a society the minority makes decisions and the majority obeys. This is an obvious truism with no power to explain political relationships. That fewer people issue laws, orders and instructions than receive and obey them is a fact scarcely worth commenting upon. The elitist argument is a much stronger one. It is that the dominant minority cannot be controlled by the majority, whatever democratic mechanisms are used. As Michels phrased it:

> Historical evolution mocks all the prophylactic measures that have been adopted for the prevention of oligarchy. If laws are passed to control the dominion of the leaders, it is the laws which gradually weaken, and not the leaders.[2]

No mechanism for ensuring the accountability of the leaders to the public, no ideology which enshrines the principle of majority will can prevent the elite from imposing its supremacy over the rest of society.

Because of their power, their organisation, their political skill or their personal qualities, the members of the elite are always potentially capable of exploiting their positions so as to preserve the elite's domination. An implication of this is that the supposed elite constitutes a coherent, united and self-conscious group – and these qualities appear in nearly all definitions. Indeed, what James Meisel calls the 'three Cs'[3]– group consciousness, coherence and conspiracy (the last term meaning a 'common will to action' rather than 'secret machinations') – are clearly necessary features of the concept of an elite.[4] To be of any relevance to a study of political influence the group must act together as a group, with some shared purposes. If the elite is the elite of the wealthy or of the products of private education they must act together as the wealthy or as the defenders of the private sector in education in order to count as an elite in politics. If the group does not act as a unified body it is less an elite than a category of 'top persons' in the particular sphere in question – the category of the 'most wealthy men' in the USA or the category of 'public school products' in Britain. The unity of the elite is sometimes seen as the outcome of the elite's social background and sometimes the product of the very organisation of the elite itself – an *esprit de corps* arising from their common situation and interests, and joint action of the group. Power breeds consciousness of power. This is commonly alleged of bureaucracies. In every case the cohesiveness of the elite is seen as one of its chief strengths.

These qualities of self-consciousness, coherence and unity are held to rein-force the advantageous position of the elite in its relations with each other groups in the society. The elitists regard power as cumulative. Power gives access to more power. As Thomas Hobbes put it in the seventeenth century: "...the nature of power, is in this point, like to fame, increasing as it proceeds; or like the motion of heavy bodies, which the further they go make still the more haste".[5] The elit-ists' conception of power, or, at least, of the use the elite will make of power, comes very close to Hobbes's definition of power as a "present means to some future apparent good". Power is a means to obtain other social goods – wealth, economic influence, social status, educational advantages for their children. In turn these, as Hobbes also pointed out, become themselves powers – wealth makes for greater wealth and for access to political power, a group's social prestige adds weight to its political activities. Both wealth and educational opportunities will tend to maintain the elite's domination in subsequent generations, converting it into a hereditary caste. These advantages of *positions déjà prises*, as Mosca termed them, serve to increase the distance between the elite and other groups. They emphasise the exclusiveness of the elite and the difficulty of obtaining entry into it on any other than the elite's own terms. The strength of the elite is in many respects indicated by its ability to lay down the terms for admission to the circle of the politically influential, terms which may include conformity to standards of wealth, social background, educational attainment and commitment to the elite's interests and ideology. On the other hand the elite's survival may, as we shall see, depend on its capacity to adjust to pressures from outside itself and even to admit elements from other social interests into the elite.

The size of the elite envisaged by elitists depends on where they draw the line between the politically influential and the less influential. Several elitists distinguish between two levels or strata within the elite. Such a distinction appears in Mosca, Pareto and Mills. Though each of these writers draws the distinction between the upper and lower levels of the elite in a somewhat different way, this common pat-tern is significant. It represents an attempt by the elitists to take into account differ-ences both in the degree and the type of influence which the various members of the elite may possess. In some cases the lower stratum of the elite is a bridge between the core of decision-makers and the rest of society. It mediates between the rulers and the ruled by transmitting information in either direction and by providing expla-nations and justifications for elite policy. It may also be the source from which the higher elite is recruited as well as the level at which outsiders first enter elite circles from below. Mosca provides the fullest instance of such a process:

> Below the highest stratum in the ruling class there is always...another that is more numerous and comprises all the capacities for leadership in the country. Without such a class any sort of social organisation would be impossible.[6]

The upper stratum of political decision-makers is insufficient in strength and num-bers to perform the great range and variety of leadership functions necessary in a society. Decisions and legislation issued by the leaders have to be explained and justified to the rest of the society. The opinion leaders who perform this task are drawn from the lower stratum of the ruling class:

> From within it comes the committees that direct political groupings, the speakers who address assemblies and meetings, the men who make and publish the newspapers and, finally, that small number of persons who are capable of forming opinions of their own as to people and events of the day, and therefore exercise great influence on the many who are not capable of having opinions of their own and are ready, perhaps without knowing it, always to follow the opinions of others.[7]

The upper stratum's decisions and laws also require execution. In a society of any complexity this task falls to the bureaucracy. Mosca suggests that the bureaucracy will be recruited from the lower stratum of the ruling class. Entry to the civil service requires education and this is more easily secured by those born into the second stratum particularly where that stratum has a tradition both of state service and of culture in general. In this way the civil service becomes impregnated with the values of the ruling class, thereby strengthening the grip that class has upon the state machine.

The second stratum, which Mosca on occasion identifies with the middle class, is, finally, the source of recruitment for the upper stratum. Mosca holds that the key to the stability of any political system lies more in the quality of the lower level of the elite than in the "few dozen persons who control the state machine". He draws an analogy with the relative importance to an army of its generals and its officer corps. If all the generals were to be lost it would be a severe blow to the army, but they could be rapidly replaced from the officer corps. But if the officers were lost the army would disintegrate. In the same way the cohesion of a society depends on the lower stratum of the elite which provides the leadership material for the society as well as the essential linkage with those who are led. The simple fact, though one which presents grave complications for the elitist standpoint, that those who take the 'decisions' in a society do not comprise all those who have 'influence' gives rise to the similar distinction between elite levels in the elite theory of C. Wright Mills. Mills distinguishes between an 'inner core' and the 'outer fringes' of the 'power elite'.[8] The inner core is made up of the men who are 'in' on the major decisions, whilst the outer members are 'those who count', whose views and interests have to be considered and conciliated by the inner core even where they do not actively participate in a given decision.

Pareto's suggested division of the elite is on a different basis. The 'governing elite' is composed of all political influentials, whether they exercise this influence directly or indirectly. It could include members of the government and of an opposition party as well as industrialists, labour leaders, military personnel or any others in the society, to the extent that they made an impact on political decision-making. The 'non-governing elite' consists of the leaders in any of the many and varied activities which do not affect political issues.

With the exception of Mills, all those referred to here as the 'classical elitists' held that the existence of a ruling elite was a necessary feature of all societies. Only Mills confined his observations to one society at one period – the USA in the 1950s – explicitly recognising that other societies and, indeed, the same society at other periods might differ radically (and had differed) in their power structure. For Mosca and Pareto the necessary existence of ruling elites was one of the laws of politics which social science had uncovered – one of the constants that such a science must seek. Nature, including human social nature, was uniform. Men were moved by the same passions and interests in the present as they had been in the past. As a consequence, patterns of social and political conduct were, in essentials, repetitive. The entire records of history stood as a storehouse of evidence as to man's political experience. Such notions were characteristic of what James Burnham was to term 'Machiavellianism'.[9] Elitists such as Mosca and Pareto saw their hypothesis as to the inevitability of minority rule confirmed at every point in history. Within the overall pattern of elitist rule history offered evidence of lesser-patterns – the existence of a limited range of types of elite, a repeated pattern of social movements whereby elites were replaced or renewed, a constant relation between the power-structure of an epoch and the prevalent political philosophies. Equally the assumption of the uniformity of nature permitted the elitists to predict the futility of egalitarian attempts, such as those of the Marxists, to establish a classless society. Elites were not merely features of all hitherto existing societies but of every society that might conceivably exist in the future.

Within the general thesis of elitism the 'classical elitists' displayed important differences. The most crucial of these differences was as to the qualities and social opportunities a group needed to possess if it were to gain an elite position. Four broad positions may be discerned, to be examined in turn. Firstly, there were those who, like Mosca and his disciple Michels, held that an elite owed its power predominantly to its organisational abilities. Pareto and his followers, by contrast, traced the elite's position to the psychological make-up of both elite and non-elite, this being in turn explicable in terms of certain constancies in human nature. James Burnham, attempting a marriage between elitism and Marxism, saw the power of the elite as a consequence of its control of economic resources, and finally C. Wright Mills similarly explained the elite's dominance not as a product of the personal qualities of its members but of the positions they held in a number of key institutions within the society.

MOSCA AND MICHELS: AN ORGANISATIONAL APPROACH

Mosca, joint author with Pareto of 'classical elitism', gave, in a famous passage, the most concise statement of the general elitist position:

Among the constant facts and tendencies that are to be found in all political organisms, one is so obvious that it is apparent to the most casual eye. In all societies…two classes of people appear – a class that rules and a class that is ruled. The first class, always the less numerous, performs all political functions, monopolises power and enjoys the advantages that power brings, whereas the second, the more numerous class, is directed and controlled by the first, in a manner that is now more or less legal, now more or less arbitrary and violent, and supplies the first, in appearance at least, with material means of subsistence and with the instrumentalities that are essential to the vitality of the political organism.[10]

Neither one man nor the mass of the people (Aristotle's 'the one' and 'the many') can rule. The single ruler needs the backing of advisers and administrators, propagandists and police. On the other side 'the people' can only act politically under the direction of a small group of leaders.

The evidence for this position Mosca drew from all periods of history. This he could allow himself to do because of his assumption of the uniformity of human nature and of the resultant social patterns.[11] Mosca, like other adherents of the 'Machiavellian' position, ignores the fact of historical development not only in material terms but also in human experience and thought. To most historians since the mid-eighteenth century it has been the dissimilarity of past action and thinking which has seemed the most striking feature of human history and which has made 'learning from the past' a dubious undertaking in both practical conduct and social analysis. Mosca's use of the term 'the historical method' to describe his practice of adducing instances of his general law from societies as varied as China, Russia, Italy and Britain and periods as far apart as the fifth century BC and the nineteenth century AD would seem a misnomer, if history is taken to be concerned, rather, with the individuality of particular epochs and societies and with the detailed process of their transformation. Mosca's attempt is better regarded as an early essay in comparative political sociology, aiming to make general statements about political regimes. It offers a typology of governments but one which is vitiated, as so many such enterprises are, by being at too high a level of generality through ignoring the historical circumstances which differentiate the regimes which it attempts to bring under a single law or a single type. China or ancient Rome are cited in support of tendencies which Mosca recognises as developing in the democracies of his own day.

The key to elite control lay for Mosca in a minority's capacity for organisation. Elite position comes as a result of its members possessing, either in fact or in the estimation of others in the society, some attribute which is valued in the society. The attribute may be wealth, a concern for the public good, military prowess or status in a religious hierarchy. Elite *control*, however, depends on the minority's capacity to weld itself into a cohesive force presenting a common front to the other forces in society. A minority, Mosca believes, has advantages simply because it is a minority.[12]

A small group is more readily organised than a large one. Its internal channels of communication and information are much simpler. Its members can be contacted more speedily. As a result, a small minority can formulate policies rapidly, can agree on the presentation of the policies and give the appearance of complete solidarity in its public statements and actions. Changed circumstances can produce an immediate response from a group which is well organised, whilst its less well organised rivals or the largely unorganised bulk of the population flounder in search of the appropriate reaction. The ultimate in elite leadership will be that the majority looks to the elite for the right 'cue' when the majority finds itself in conditions unfamiliar to it.

The consequence is that despite the apparent superiority of a majority over a minority, in any concrete situation it will be the minority that will be the stronger. The unorganised majority will be merely a large aggregation of individuals without a common purpose or any generally acknowledged system of communicating information or coordinating policy. As Mosca puts it, "The power of any minority is irresistible as against each single individual in the majority, who stands alone before the totality of the organised minority".[13]

As we have seen Mosca's elite or ruling class – his own term was 'political class' – was subdivided into a higher and a lower stratum. Influenced by the growing power in his day of the party machine Mosca regarded the innermost core of the elite as comprising the party 'bosses' who directed the party's electoral campaigns and thereby controlled the parliament. These 'grand electors', as Mosca terms them,[14] not only deliver the vote in the electoral area where their power is based but, most importantly, they pick the candidates. They determine the range from which the electorate must make its supposedly 'free choice'.

A representative is thus not chosen by the electorate. Instead 'his friends have him elected'[15] and hence – an excellent instance of Mosca's thesis – "a candidacy is always the work of a group of people united for a common purpose, an organised minority which inevitably forces its will upon the disorganised majority".[16] Such party bosses, existing, as they did, behind the scenes and having no constitutional or legal standing, were in no way accountable to the electorate. The representatives are the mere tools of the bosses.

One consequence that Mosca drew in his earlier writings[17] was that no man of principle and integrity would agree to stand for election. The representatives would, instead, be of mediocre ability. The assembly would be lowered in quality and would cease to represent the full range of interests amongst the ruling class. As Meisel points out, Mosca faced a dilemma of reconciling this tendency with the faith he placed in the middle class, as a source of political regeneration. Mosca never resolved the problem and, perhaps for this reason, let the issue of the decline in the political leadership drop quietly from his later treatment in *The Ruling Class*, where the elected political leadership takes on a higher status than Mosca accorded them in his youthful writings. In the interim, as we shall see, he had come to reassess the value of representative democracy in general – and had become a representative himself.

Although Mosca holds that every society will be dominated by a ruling class this does not imply that there are no substantial differences between political systems. They differ in two main respects – the direction of the flow of authority and the source of recruitment to the ruling class.[18] These offer two axes along which political systems may be arranged for purposes of comparison. Mosca discerned two 'principles' according to which authority flowed and two 'tendencies' according to which elite membership was recruited. Authority in any political organisation, Mosca asserted, either flows downward – the 'autocratic principle' – or upward – the 'liberal principle'. In an autocracy officials are appointed and granted authority by some higher official. In a liberal system the rulers are authorised by those ruled – usually by means of election. 'Autocracy' and 'liberal' are 'ideal types' of systems of authority to which any given society will conform to a greater or lesser degree. Many will be mixtures of these principles. Mosca cites the USA where the chief executive derives his authority by the liberal principle of election but where the other executive heads are appointed by him according to the principle of autocracy.

Recruitment of the ruling class will, Mosca suggests, display either 'aristocratic' or a 'democratic' tendency. The tendency is aristocratic when new members of the ruling class are recruited from the descendants of the existing ruling class – a disposition which all ruling classes share. The democratic tendency is displayed where the ruling class is renewed from the lower class of those ruled. Both these tendencies are ever present in political systems but vary in intensity from time to time and place to place with the aristocratic tendency sometimes prevailing and at other times the democratic. In its extreme form each tendency has its dangers. A society which is overwhelmingly aristocratic will tend ultimately to stultify with its ruling class losing contact with the needs and interests of the society. The opposite extreme – where the democratic tendency is completely dominant – logically designates a revolutionary situation. A ruling class scarcely exists since it is in the process of replacement from below. Clearly, on Mosca's analysis, this position would rapidly stabilise itself since the revolutionary lower classes are always led by a minority which inevitably converts itself into a new ruling class. Normally the democratic tendency is more moderate – a process of very gradual infiltration of the ruling class by individuals from the lower class. Such a moderated democratic tendency may even be interpreted as a conservative force. It permits the ruling class to be renewed and rejuvenated by being brought into contact with the interests and aspirations of the ruled. By this means the ablest amongst those ruled are recruited for the ruling class, thus preventing a decline in the quality of leadership it provides.[19]

Mosca's two principles of authority and his two tendencies of recruitment may

Figure 1: *Flow of authorisation 'principles'*

		Autocratic	Liberal
Source (flow) of recruitment 'tendencies'	Aristocratic		
	Democratic		

be combined in any of four ways – thus offering the basis for comparative political analysis. An autocratic system of authority is most often discovered to be combined with an aristocratic method of recruitment into the ruling class. Hereditary
monarchy tends to appoint its officialdom from amongst the hereditary nobility.
But some autocracies display a 'democratic' tendency in recruitment to the ruling
class appointing to positions of authority according to merit regardless of social or
economic origins. Mosca cites the mandarinate of China and the Roman Catholic
Church as instances.

Similarly political systems where authority comes from below – observe the
liberal principle – may show either an aristocratic or a democratic tendency in
their patterns of recruitment to the ruling class. 'Liberal' societies where authority depends on election have frequently either confined the electorate to the hereditary aristocracy – as in the Polish constitution – or else have regularly re-elected
members of aristocratic 'political families'. Finally the liberal principle may com-
bine with the democratic tendency where, as in a modern representative democracy such as Britain, persons from all classes are elected to positions of authority.
Mosca is, however, committed to holding – though he is not explicit on the point
– that this last combination is in part an illusion. Whilst it is true that a 'liberal-
democratic' system may recruit to positions of authority persons from any socio-
economic class, the elections, as we have seen, do not offer a free choice but one
manipulated by the political elite. This political elite, moreover, will tend, whatever its social origins, to convert itself into a hereditary ruling class. It is implicit
in Mosca's argument that the overall trend of political systems must be to gravi-
tate to either the aristocratic-autocratic or the aristocratic-liberal type.

In his later work Mosca openly stated what he conceived the ideal situation to
be, abandoning the show of scientific neutrality that he had paraded in his earliest
writing. The stance he adopted was a liberal-conservative one of long ancestry
dating back, as Meisel has pointed out, to Aristotle whose political science Mosca
had originally set out to refute. A balance between the principles and tendencies
was desirable – with enough democratic openness to refresh the ruling class and
enough of an aristocratic restrictiveness to ensure stability, a 'liberal' system of
elective authority but an electorate confined to the middle class led by the "little
nucleus of sound minds and choice spirits that keep mankind from going to the
dogs every other generation".[20]

These openly prescriptive passages form part of the later Mosca's conclusions
from his academic and practical political experience. They are drawn from the
second volume of Mosca's *Elementi di scienza politica* published in 1923 and
written after World War 1. Mosca had, by this time, come to a more favourable
opinion of representative government and this is reflected in the sociological
analysis he offers of the ruling class in such a system. The standpoint is much
more pluralistic. The ruling class incorporates the leaderships of the plurality of
interest groups or 'social forces' which affect major decision-making in the society. Such forces may well have rival aims with now one group dominant and now
another according to social and economic circumstance or the skill of the group's

leadership. The ruling class in a representative democracy may even be divided into two or more parties competing with one another for the votes of the electorate.

In this later and 'weaker' version of elite theory the 'three Cs' – consciousness, cohesiveness and conspiracy – are almost abandoned, and Mosca's ruling class appears, as a consequence, to be a mere category of 'top people'. The ruling class is now implicitly defined in terms of the extent of the political influence of the individuals and groups within it rather than in terms of its unity and exclusiveness. Membership of the class is attained and maintained by skill in manipulating the balance between the ruling groups and in exploiting the aspirations of the mass electorate. This wider electorate, composed of the poorer and less educated sections of the population, will be 'used' by the battling elements in the ruling class in their struggle for power. This will involve their making at least partial concessions to what Mosca believed to be the mediocre moral standards and ignorant economic and political demands of the bulk of the population. This indirect influence of the masses on the ruling class leads only to corruption of political life – a view taken by many nineteenth century liberal-conservatives.

Mosca's own solution was also that of a period liberal. He now defends representative government as the most effective means of articulating interests in a society, of utilising the talents of a country and of permitting the abler elements of the governed classes to enter the ruling class.[21] Representative government permits the electorate to balance the liberal authority of parliament against the autocratic authority of bureaucracy. The ruling class, Mosca believed, should assume a greater importance in providing moral leadership in the community. It should be a class of public-spirited persons, not all of whom would hold upper-stratum positions of power, who should all contribute to guiding the community towards the public interest. Mosca would restore to the ruling class its cohesiveness and self-consciousness but this should be a consciousness of its common responsibility to the society. "It must become aware that it is a ruling class, and so gain a clear conception of its rights and duties".[22]

Mosca supports a reform which had been central to much liberal thought of the nineteenth century. This was the decentralisation of government which would enable a larger number of the educated middle class – Mosca's lower stratum – to participate in public life, on a voluntary basis, as justices of the peace, as members of regional administrative bodies and so on. The aim was to translate the English gentry class into twentieth century terms. Mosca even hankered after restricting the franchise to the lower stratum of the ruling class[23] but was forced to conclude that it was too late to rectify the 'mistake' of granting universal suffrage.[24] Mosca's elitism finally sheds its scientific clothing and is revealed as ideology – a political theory for the middle class.

In the main work of Mosca's disciple, Robert Michels, the ideological content is kept more firmly under control. Michels treats more methodically, in *Political Parties*, theories which Mosca had proposed but not fully developed. Once again the central theme is that elite control depends upon organisation. Michels extends this to mean not merely that organisational ability grants power but that the very structure of any organised society gives rise inevitably to an elite. In Michels' celebrated formulation: "Who says organization, says oligarchy".[25]

Michels' method of investigation was, perhaps, the most rigidly 'scientific' of any of the 'classical' elitists. He proposed a hypothetical law governing all social organisations – the celebrated 'iron law of oligarchy' – and then proceeded to test the hypothesis by examining the organisation which *prima facie* seemed to constitute the outstanding counter-examples to the law. The organisations studied were the socialist parties of Europe in the years before the war and in particular the German socialist party. These parties were dedicated to preserving equality and democracy in their internal organisation. They regarded their leaders as mere agents of the mass party. Sovereignty within the party lay with the conference of the party composed of elected delegates. The parties devised machinery such as frequent elections, to ensure that "the party leads and the leaders follow". Leadership was constantly distrusted, particularly middle-class intellectual leadership in what were basically proletarian parties. It is, however, Michels' contention that even such organisations, devoted to the negation of any tendency towards elite control, nevertheless display the 'iron law of oligarchy'.

Michels never offered a precise formulation of the law of oligarchy but its meaning is clear.[26] In any organisation of any size leadership becomes necessary to its success and survival. The nature of organisation is such that it gives power and advantages to the group of leaders who cannot then be checked or held accountable by their followers. This is true despite the fact that where the leadership is elected the leaders are supposedly the agents of those electing them. There are sets of factors which cause this result – organisational factors and psychological. Of these the organisational factors are by far the most significant.

Michels argues that as soon as human cooperative activities attain the size and complexity which warrant the term 'organisation', technical expertise is required if the enterprise is not to founder. Like Max Weber before him, Michels insists that attempts at control of an organisation by the mass of its members involves an amateurishness totally self-defeating in an age of large-scale organisation. A political party campaigning to gain power needs to organise its vote, canvass supporters, supply information for speakers, raise contributions, attend to the party's financial structure and its legal standing. It needs to establish a coordinated policy line for the sake of consistency and solidarity. All these activities require expertise which the mass of members may not have the aptitude to develop and for which they certainly lack the leisure. Mass control conflicts with efficiency and is replaced by professional direction both in policy-making and in technical administration. The result of this 'technical indispensability of leadership' is that control of the party passes into the hands of its leading politicians and its bureaucracy.

Michels then demonstrates that power breeds power – a central tenet of elitism. The leadership controls the party funds and the party's channels of information – notably its newspaper – it attempts to select parliamentary candidates, it dispenses patronage. Its activities are news, publicised even by the opposition press.

An important feature in Michels' analysis is his recognition of the impact that the party's role in the whole political system of the society has on the internal power structure of the party. Power for the party necessitates electoral success. Electoral success, however, requires the support of voters who are not necessarily party members – people who are less committed to party principle, who are on the 'margin' of the party. To gain their allegiance the party must moderate its dogma, must provide continuity of leadership to give an assurance of stability, must devote itself to organising its vote rather than maintaining the purity of its doctrine.

These factors, Michels suggests, strengthen the hands of two groups. Firstly, it strengthens the expert party bureaucrats more interested in the technique of power than concerned with principle. Secondly, it strengthens the elected parliamentary representatives of the party whose election gives them added weight within the party, but who owe their electoral success to their appeal to the electorate at large rather than to the much narrower party membership. The party leaders thus owe their power within the party in large part to their support outside the party. The party members cannot readily depose the leadership without damaging the party's electoral standing.

Ultimately the party is forced to adopt a hierarchy which mirrors the hierarchical power structure in the political system as a whole with 'shadow' ministers supported by an efficient bureaucracy. Mass control is discovered to be incompatible with political power and so oligarchy triumphs, with the leadership proven to be 'stable and irremovable'. Even the attempts to maintain a proletarian leadership for the proletarian parties and thus prevent the estrangement between leader and led is, Michels insists, foredoomed to failure. Instead a 'proletarian elite' emerges which ceases to be proletarian in anything but origin as it exchanges manual for desk work and wages for salary. The leaders are 'bourgeoisified', strangers to their class, and the party hierarchy becomes an established career offering a rise in social status as well as income.[27]

These organisational and structural forces pushing towards oligarchy are reinforced, in Michels' view, by certain psychological forces, largely of a negative kind. Whilst socialist theorists have often assumed a high degree of political interest and spontaneity on the part of the bulk of the population, Michels alleges that the majority is apathetic towards public matters. Most people are only concerned with politics when it affects their private interests. They have no knowledge of how the political system works. The same applies to the members of party organisations. There is a small inner group who constitute the party active and are the truly influential. Below this group activity, interest and influence in the party may be represented by a pyramid – voluntary party officials, a larger stratum of those regularly attending meetings, a larger stratum still of enrolled members and, finally, a large basis of non-members who merely vote for the party.

For Michels, apathy goes with technical incompetence in political matters. Political knowledge has to be organised to be effective and in Michels' description the majority is too apathetic to organise itself. Such men have, he believes, a psychological need for guidance.[28] They are glad to have others take on political responsibilities. Even revolutionary agitation has to be undertaken by a small minority on their behalf. Such apathy, submissiveness and deference provide ideal conditions for the few with the interest and the organisational ability to lead.

Though Michels confines his particular analysis to political parties the law of oligarchy is intended to have general application to all organisation including the organisation of the state as such. The majority will never rule despite the formal apparatus of universal suffrage and the myths of majority will. Democracy in the sense of the rule of the whole people or of the majority is impossible. In any democracy the major decisions will be taken by a powerful oligarchy. But Michels comes round to a limited defence of democracy.[29] It allows the emergence of a number of rival parties – each led by an oligarchy – whose competition ensures a certain amount of indirect influence to the people whose support they must cultivate. The democratic tendency restrains but cannot prevent the oligarchical. As with Mosca elitism makes a compromise with pluralism when democracy is defined in terms of the competition between oligarchies.[30]

PARETO: A PSYCHOLOGICAL APPROACH

Pareto's system, as expounded most fully in the *Treatise of General Sociology* (*The Mind and Society*), is the grandest of all the classical elitist doctrines – a "gargantuan retort to Marx" as its latest commentator has described it.[31] The elite is painted with much broader brush-strokes than in any other of the elitists' works. Pareto's elite can be much wider and more comprehensive than the political bosses whom Mosca or Michels study, sometimes wider even than Marx's ruling class. Pareto's elite theory is part of a much more general sociology in which social activity is explained by reference to certain fundamental psychological factors. Accordingly elites are seen by Pareto not as the product of economic forces nor as building their dominance on their organisational ability but as the outcome of what Pareto believed to be human attributes constant throughout history.

Pareto's first definition of an elite in the *Treatise* is, however, a highly formal one. He suggests that ability in every human activity – law, poetry, thieving – might, at least in theory, be measured and each practitioner awarded marks according to his success.[32] The top lawyer would be awarded ten and the one who cannot get a brief would be given zero. A 'great train robber' is marked at ten if he gets away with the money and the petty thief caught in the act gains no marks. The evaluation is not a moral one but is a measurement of displayed achievement. Pareto then proposes to make a class of the persons with the highest indices in each branch of activity and to call this class the 'elite'.[33] This elite is then subdivided into those who directly or indirectly play an important part in government – termed the 'governing elite' – and those, like top chess-players, whose activities are not significant for politics – the 'non-governing elite'. Pareto rapidly abandons this formal definition as impractical for sociological research. Only in theoretical conditions of perfect competition is it true that those with the highest ability reach the top of their activity. In practice this does not always happen. Factors such as wealth, birth and corruption frequently give advantages to the less skilled to attain the leading positions, particularly in such less technical and rational activities as politics.

Pareto resorts instead to a simpler distinction between the elite (governing and non-governing) defined as those who, regardless of ability, in fact occupy the leading positions and the non-elite. Paralleling Marx's account of history in terms of class struggle, Pareto sees the history of every hitherto-existing society as the history of the relations between its elite and its non-elite and of the psychological make-up of the elite. Pareto believed that the vast majority of human activities were 'non-logical', i.e. were not rational in the sense of appearing to the actor and to an impartial observer both to be consciously undertaken to reach an attainable end and to be appropriate to that end.

Usually, however, men attempt to justify their conduct by giving it a 'veneer of logic'. If these theories or rationalisations are analysed they will be found to be composed of two elements. One part is the justification itself which, however apparently logical, is nevertheless part of non-logical conduct. It varies from time to time and from country to country. It is termed by Pareto the 'derivation' and is the counterpart of Marx's 'ideology'. The other part of the theory is more important. It is the direct reflection of the instincts or sentiments or state of mind of the actor, and are called by Pareto 'residues', Human instincts, and hence the residues which reflect them, are, Pareto believes, constant throughout history.

Pareto discerned a number of important residues, most of which he finally subsumed under two classes which offered the key to the explanation of society including elite domination and elite replacement. Class I residues reflect the 'instinct of combinations' – the impulse to put together ideas by the use of imagination. Arts, ideologies and political coalitions and manoeuvrings would all stem from this active, inventive instinct. Class II residues reflect the instinct of 'the persistence of aggregates'– the tendency to consolidate positions once they are established. Class II residues are manifestations of instincts for permanence, stability and order. They appear politically in appeals for solidarity, order, discipline, property or family. They must not, however, be identified with traditionalism – one may have stable attachments to new or even revolutionary movements.

It is the distribution of these residues or their corresponding instincts in the society that is crucially important. Men have a predominance of either Class I residues – men of intelligence and cunning, 'foxes' in Machiavelli's language – or of Class II – men of strength, stability and integrity, 'lions'. The two sets of qualities are mutually exclusive. Politics, however, requires both the lion and the fox – it is partly a matter of force and partly one of persuasion, meaning in Pareto's view gaining the consent of the governed by ruse. The style of governing at any time will depend on whether the governing elite is composed predominantly of those with Class I or those with Class II residues. The non-elite are overwhelmingly 'Class II' in character – stolid, unimaginative but also with strong attachments to political ideals which satisfy their need for stable commitments. Hence the appeal of religions from Christianity to imperialism and socialism.

'Foxes' govern by attempting to gain consent. They devise ideologies to attract the masses, construct policies to meet immediate crises and satisfy the demand of the moment. Material interest is placed before the pursuit of ideals. The ideal politician is the political fixer or 'wheeler-dealer'. 'Foxes' are not, however, prepared to use force to resolve political problems. Misplaced humanitarianism leads to compromise and pacifism which fatally weaken the regime when the ultimate manoeuvre has failed to deceive the elite's more tough-minded opponents. The 'lions' manner of governing represents the opposite pole in political styles. The pursuit of consensus is abandoned in favour of the use of force. Opposition may be ruthlessly suppressed. Public order rather than private satisfaction becomes a chief end of government. Such elites are far from lacking in ideals, however. Violence, including the forceful overthrow of a previous 'Class I elite', may be used to defend religion and morality against 'materialism', 'atheism' or 'corruption'. Many a revolutionary military regime makes such claims. Pareto, contemptuous as he was of what he believed to be the corruption, sterile manoeuvrings and political cowardice of the continental democracies of his day, rejoiced in the use of violence by the men of action – the Caesars and the Mussolinis.[34] He wastes no sympathy on the victims who are merely indices of the courage and strength of the men of decision who are "ridding the country of a baneful animal pest". A balance of the qualities of lion and fox was Pareto's ideal – as it had been for Machiavelli – but this was extremely rare in an elite. As a result the balance swings in history from one elite-type to the other.[35]

Pareto's elite, it can be seen, is identified by the attitudes it shares and the conduct these give rise to. Pareto, like Marx and for not very dissimilar reasons, is ambiguous as to the degree of cohesion an elite possesses. Mcisel's 'three Cs' – consciousness, cohesion and conspiracy – are less readily attributable to it, particularly in modern democracies. Indeed the objection might be made to Pareto's account that it is at times a description of a category of 'top persons' rather than an elite as it has been defined here. Pareto rejects the 'conspiracy theory' of society.[36] In modern democracies, for instance, any accord between the actions of the Class I elite is a result of each 'fox' taking independent decisions in pursuit of his own interest. But it is also possible that the aggregate of individual actions may not accord with the long-term interests of the elite. Pareto saw, as Marx had done, that social actions can have unforeseen and unintended consequences. The lack of conspiracy and cohesion is evidenced by the ease with which one elite is displaced by another as a result of a host of individual actions which ultimately undermine the position of the elite. 'Foxes' and 'lions' fail to recognise the disastrous consequences to themselves of, respectively, their tender-mindedness and their stolid inflexibility.

In a democracy Pareto's elite is broad enough to include the rival leaderships of the political parties. Only those totally opposed to the regime and unwilling to compromise by participating in it can be counted as outside the elite. Tested by the standard of their actions, attitudes and ideologies the 'constitutional oppositions'

displayed identical Class I residues with the holders of office, being equally prepared to play the game of governing by ruse. Interest groups such as unions, and
employers who also play the democratic game by competing for a share in the
national product, are all, for the same reason, part of the one elite. Pareto's picture
of the elite under democracy is not, then, of a cohesive group of businessmen,
politicians and bureaucrats acting in collusion. As in Marx, however, a conspiratorial element is not altogether missing from the account. The Class I elite may be
composed of competing groups but Pareto also refers to an inner core of the elite
which appears to exercise a more conscious control at least in the short run
(§§2254-2259; 2267). This it does more by its skill in distributing favours, adjusting to the turns of economic and political fortune than by its control of the instruments of coercion. The extent to which the 'three Cs' can be attributed to Pareto's
elite will depend, therefore, on whether it is this inner group or the wider elite that
is under discussion.

Pareto's typology of political systems is, therefore, basically two-fold. All are
oligarchies but in some elites Class I residues predominate while in others Class
II residues prevail. Pareto also recognises the existence of mixed types where
either a Class II elite has been infiltrated by men of Class I residues or a basically Class I elite is backed by a proportion of Class II elements. These mixed
regimes tend, however, to revert to one or other of the 'pure' types and can be
regarded as sub-types. Pareto cites a great deal of historical evidence in favour of
his schema and it is not difficult to think of further instances of the tender-minded and cunning or the tough-minded and idealistic political conduct he describes.
The scheme is, however, inadequate on a number of accounts. It suggests affini-
ties between regimes otherwise different but it does not explain the differences
which are at least as striking. Pareto's faith in the uniformity of human nature permits him to classify the democracy of Athens in the fifth century BC as belonging
to the same type as the mass democracies of modern Europe because of their common possession of 'Class I elites'. The great contrasts between the two systems in
their political institutions, scale of operation, degree of bureaucratisation and economic structure are ignored in favour of the one alleged similarity.

The basis for claiming such uniformities is in itself highly disputable. Pareto
offers no satisfactory reasons for accepting his view that 'residues', as the constants, are more significant historically than the ideologies they give rise to, nor
does he recognise that the 'residues' themselves may assume different meanings
in different political and intellectual contexts. To say that the leadership of ancient
Athens and that in modern democracy both display cunning tells us little about the
kinds of policies or manoeuvres each will undertake. In short, Pareto ignores the
findings of the historians, sociologists and anthropologists who since the mid-
eighteenth century have studied the process of social differentiation and the effect
of environment in altering human responses.

Finally, the concept of the 'residue' is not subjected to a very stringent analysis. It usefully distinguishes certain patterns of political actions – even if it under-
rates their historical uniqueness. Much political conduct is ambiguous if examined

in the light of Pareto's dichotomy between classes of residue. Is the elite's appeal to austerity in a time of crisis a display of its Class II residues or of the cunning of a 'fox' who has perceived a way of satisfying the idealism of the mass? Pareto offers no way of deciding. Nor, most crucially of all, does he prove that residues exist. Instead, he infers their existence from the historical actions and political patterns which the residues are supposed to have caused or which are alleged to be the result of the distribution of his two psychological types. The cunning of the ancient Athenian elite is demonstration of the existence of Class I residues and, at the same time, the conduct of the Athenian elite is explained by the existence of the residues. In other words one demonstrates the existence of residues by the facts of history and explains the facts of history by reference to the residues thus discovered.[37]

BURNHAM: AN ECONOMIC APPROACH

We saw in the previous chapter that elitism set out to displace the Marxian theory of the ruling class. Marxists, in turn, dismiss elitism as bourgeois ideology. Despite this there have been attempts to demonstrate that the two theories are at least complementary and may even be fruitfully combined. Of such attempts James Burnham's *The Managerial Revolution*, which appeared in 1941, is the one with the greatest aspirations to being a system in the elitist tradition. Burnham himself was to publish one of the most popular expositions of elitist thought only two years later under the title *The Machiavellians*. Burnham's contention in *The Managerial Revolution* was that the capitalist system was in decline and would be replaced by a society controlled economically and politically by a managerial elite. For the moment the accuracy of this assessment is of less importance to our purpose than Burnham's method of establishing his position. Burnham's first assumptions are derived from the elitists – that politics is always a matter of struggle between groups for power and status and that in all societies a small group will inevitably control ultimate decision-making. Social change occurs as a result of a shift in the composition of the elite – an old elite replaced by a new one. An egalitarian, classless society is inconceivable in the conditions of advanced industrialised societies with their need for technical training and expertise. The failure of the Bolshevik revolution in Russia to establish such a society was proof to Burnham that a new class of rulers must inevitably arise.

Burnham is, however, Marxist in his understanding of where the basis of any elite's power must lie. It is control over the chief means of production which gives a group a dominant position in any society. Control has two aspects. The controlling group will prevent others gaining 'access' to the means of production and it will receive 'preferential treatment' when the product – in money or goods – is distributed.[38] These two forms of control normally go together. It is, Burnham suggests, a sign of stress in a society if control of access does not bring with it preferential treatment and status. In normal circumstances "...the easiest way to discover what the ruling group is in any society is usually to see what group gets the biggest incomes".[39] Power, for Burnham as for both Marxists and elitists, is cumulative. Control of production gives rise to political power and social prestige as well as to wealth. State institutions are gradually integrated with the prevailing system of economic control. The laws of the state help sustain the dominance of the owners of the means of production by protecting existing property relationships. Under capitalism, according to Burnham, a separation is maintained between the state and the economy – the state not intervening with the capitalists' enterprise but establishing a legal framework within which a capitalist economic system can succeed. In the last resort, however, control over the means of production does not depend upon legal forms but upon the nature of the economy. Success or failure of the elite in perpetuating its power depends on its monopolising the instruments of production. Where it permits another group access to existing productive forces or allows it to develop novel techniques, its position will be undermined. Burnham's explanation of class change is Marxist but his assertion that the result will in all circumstances involve the re-establishment of class rule is elitist.[40]

The crisis Burnham discerned in capitalism arose out of the fact, as he saw it, that the formal 'owners' of productive forces – the capitalists – had become increasingly divorced from the actual operations of production. The capitalists, having originally been managers of their own enterprises, later left this activity to professional managers and concentrated on financing – a stage removed from the productive process. The final stage of the decline of the capitalist class was its gradual retirement even from financing to constitute a 'leisured class' spending the profits from their firms without contributing to production.[41] Meanwhile the productive process itself had come into the hands of a managerial class – a skilled technical elite with its counterparts in the state bureaucracy – whose position was, dependent, not on the capitalist finance structure, but on the technical nature of modern production to which it was essential. In Burnham's terms they controlled access to the means of production, but, whilst the capitalist system survived, preferential treatment in the distribution of resources would go to the leisured capitalists who had become an excrescence in the activity of production.

Such a 'contradiction', in Marxist terminology, cannot last. "Control over access is decisive", Burnham states, and will eventually be consolidated into complete control over the means of production including the receipt of preferential treatment. The capitalist ruling class would not, however, be overthrown in favour of a classless society but would be displaced by the technically indispensable managerial elite. Once again economic control makes for political control. Projecting forward trends he finds apparent in contemporary societies, Burnham predicts that government will increasingly be a matter of executive action rather than legislation and will be run by the bureaucrats whether civil servants in Britain, the state planners in the USSR, the heads of executive bureaux in the USA or, as Burnham partly envisaged, the administrators of the European Common Market – men more akin in outlook to the industrial managers than to the 'politicians' of the capitalist era. The capitalist dichotomy between state and economy will cease as industry becomes increasingly state-run and as managerial personnel and state bureaucrats become interchangeable with the growing similarity of their functions and methods. Managerial control of the state and state control of the economy will ultimately consolidate a new elite domination – elitism with a Marxist flavour.

C. WRIGHT MILLS: AN INSTITUTIONAL APPROACH

C. Wright Mills shares with Burnham the belief that the status and composition of an elite cannot properly be explained in terms of the talents or psychology of its individual members but must be studied in the context of the economic and social structure of the particular society. Positions of power are not carved out by 'great men' but are attached to certain roles in the society. Whereas Burnham held power in society to arise from control of the means of production, Mills sees it as attached to a wider set of institutions comprised, in the USA – to which Mills confines his attention – of the military, the big corporations and the political executive. The elite is the product of, in Mills' terms, "the institutional landscape" of the society. Power in modern society is institutionalised. Certain institutions occupy "pivotal positions" in the society and the uppermost ranks of the hierarchy in these institutions constitute the "strategic command posts of the social structure".[42] The elite is thus composed of those who hold the leading positions in the strategic hierarchies. The cohesiveness of the elite will be in large part determined by the closeness of the links between the institutional hierarchies.

> If these hierarchies are scattered and disjointed, then their respective elites tend to be scattered and disjointed; if they have many interconnections and points of coinciding interest, then their elites tend to form a coherent kind of grouping.[43]

For a national 'power elite' to exist there must, on Mills' view, be some contact between the leaders of the hierarchies. Such contact may range from conscious conspiracy to a mere consensus amongst the leaders as to policies and values. This 'institutional proximity' is at its strongest where individuals "interchange commanding roles at the top of one dominant institutional order with those in another".[44]

Mills cites as instances the numerous cases of presidents and directors of large business corporations in the USA who have taken up major posts in the government and then have returned to business or to the great foundations. The ease with which this interchange of roles is made indicates for Mills the degree of cohesiveness of the elite. The greater the degree of interchange and institutional proximity the more unified the elite.[45] Though this unity is in the first place the product of the institutional structure the normal cumulative nature of power is again evident in that the interconnections of the elites leads to a shared style of life and a sense of unity – 'consciousness' added to 'coherence'.[46] This style of life tends to be per-petuated as like recruits like. As a result the elite in the USA, though not composed of a few 'great families', is, nevertheless, recruited from the wealthier classes.[47]

Power in modern American society, for Mills, is, then, not an attribute of class-es or persons but of institutions. The power elite consists of those "... in positions to make decisions having major consequences...in command of the major hierar-chies and organisations of modern society".[48] The elite is thus described in terms of its potential power rather than the actual exercise of power. The power attached to elite positions may not in fact be used by their occupants. They may, instead, allow events to take their own course, let matters 'drift' and history be made "behind men's backs".[49] At the core of Mills' analysis – and of his political radi-calism – is, the belief that within the dominant institutions of modern US society the means for exercising power are more narrowly concentrated into a few hands than at any previous time in history. Such power is seen as the ability to "make history"[50] – the ability of one person or group to change the course of large num-bers of persons' activity in a significant way.

The history-making power of the elite is sufficient, Mills believes, to overturn the *status quo*, call into question the existing social relationship and establish a new structure. The inner core of the elite is able, potentially, to determine the roles both it and others will play in society. The major policy decisions of American government in the last generation – Mills cites the bombing of Hiroshima and the commitment to the Korean war as typical – illustrate the enormous centralisation of the means of decision-making in the hands of a very few institutional officer-holders. In the USA giant inter-related corporations have replaced the multiplici-ty of small businesses, federal government dominates the several states and cen-tralises previously scattered powers and a massive military hierarchy has grown up in place of the various state militias.[51] The final stage towards the unified power elite now threatens the USA – the interchange and integration of the elites of each hierarchy, involving "...the decisive centralisation of all the means of power and decision, which is to say – all the means of history-making".[52] The assertions of American political scientists that freedom and democratic values are safeguarded in the USA by the existence of a plurality of elites competing for popular support are shown up, Mills believes, to be part of a liberal myth. It is the concentration of elite power, not its diffusion, which is, for him, the "major clue to our condition".

THE CONCEPT OF THE MASS

The counterpart of the elite in all these theories is the 'mass'. There is much less disagreement amongst elitists as to the nature of the mass than there is as to the character of the elite. The mass is, typically, 'atomised'. Its members are not organised for concerted political action. Instead each person tends to live his own private life, concentrating on his own interests both in work and leisure. His con-tacts with others in the mass tend to be limited to the members of his family, neighbours and his immediate work associates. The narrow confines of such a life limit the individual's view of public affairs. In contrast to the elite he lacks the vantage point from which to see the whole of the social system – its movements and interactions. According to Mills the members of the mass are caught in their own 'milieux'.[53] Only the elite is able to transcend the milieu in which it finds itself and create a new environment. Only the elite in the command posts of the society gains an overall view. The perception of the mass is fragmented. It is unable to see even the purpose of its own activities since it does not see what part they play in the total structure. The man in the mass "…has no projects of his own: he fulfils the routines that exist".[54]

Such inertia is invariably part of the elitist picture of the mass. The mass is able to act as a single unit only when it is integrated from outside by the elite. Leadership can transform the mass from an aggregation of isolated units into a solid, unified group. But this unity is entirely artificial. It does not arise spontaneously from within the mass. Lenin, the elitist amongst theorists of working class revolution, demanded that the spontaneous uprisings of the workers should be consciously resisted since the workers themselves never transcend their mileux to see the distinction between bread riots and total revolution.[55] Instead the revolution should be directed by an elite of trained, professional revolutionaries able, from their central positions in the movement, to coordinate its activities. In this way otherwise meaningless isolated uprisings by the mass gained revolutionary significance. The impact and involvement of the mass was paradoxically greater as a result of the direction given by an elite of possibly a mere dozen men. Lenin indeed presses the contrast between elite and mass to its extreme limit by suggesting that without leadership there is no such coherent thing as a 'people' – there is merely a mass.

Lenin's extreme version of the dependence of mass action upon elite leadership was occasioned by the need for disciplined, secret revolutionary organisation in an autocratic police-state. Other elitists present a version of the theory for more democratic societies which is milder but not different in kind from that of Lenin. For Mosca and Michels the mass in a representative democracy was politically incompetent, apathetic and inert. The mass, because atomised, was not equipped with the wider view of the society necessary for ruling. Just as important, however, was that the mass had no desire for leadership. Far from being politically ambitious the individuals in the mass were glad to have the responsibility of decision-making taken off their shoulders. The mass displays a psychological need for guidance and direction. Even the working class movements aiming to promote mass interests collapsed without the leadership of a bourgeois oligarchy. Political initiative became the responsibility of the elite as a result, in large part, of the indifference of the mass. The elite cultivates its coherence and consciousness whilst adopting towards the mass a policy or 'divide and rule'.[56] Horizontal contacts between members of the society break down and are replaced by vertical contacts between atomised individuals and the elite. Modern totalitarian regimes using techniques of terror have been interpreted as acting in this manner to ensure the complete atomisation of the mass and to force each individual to display allegiance only to the centre.

IDEOLOGY AND SOCIAL CONTROL

No elitist claims that the elite maintains its domination over the other classes merely by the exercise of coercion. In fact the study of the coercive powers of the elite plays a very small part in elitist analysis. The elitists wish to make the far more significant point that elite rule comes to be accepted by the rest of the society. The mass, they assert, very readily acknowledges the legitimacy of the dominant minority. Accordingly the elitists deal extensively with the process by which an elite gains the support of the rest of society. The elitists in this respect studied, prophesied and promoted not so much an age of violence as an age of propaganda. Any group aspiring to power will, the elitists suggest, attempt to justify its potential activities. To do this successfully it must state its aims not in self-interested terms but in ways which will gain the acceptance of all other classes and groups in the society. It will, therefore, appeal to some set of general moral and political principles which the society at large will be prepared to acknowledge as having universal validity – as being principles which any person or group might properly follow in political dealings. Despite their appearance of universality, however, such principles promoted the particular interests of the group advocating them. What purported to be a philosophy establishing general truths was in fact an ideology protecting partial interests. It assists in binding the group together with a set of shared values. Such an ideology is not necessarily the conscious conspiratorial construction of the elite. Its members may be entirely convinced of the truth of the principles they enunciate. In fact it is a mark of the success of an ideology that it is accepted as part of the received opinion of the whole of the society, looked upon as being as normal as any feature of the natural landscape.

Examples of the many such ideologies, myths, derivations (Pareto's word) or 'political formulae' (Mosca's term) are the 'divine right of kings' and the doctrine of 'popular will' in modern democracy.[57] The political impact of divine right theories depended on the widespread acceptance of a religious belief in a divine world order in which kings like angels, ordinary men and animals each had their appointed place. Acceptance of such a belief involved the recognition of the legitimacy of kingship. In the modern era the will of the majority is defended as the proper technique for political decision-making by appealing to the higher universally acknowledged principle of 'the equality of man'. Here the faith in the principle of equality blinds men to the fact of inequality. The falsity of the belief is, however, no bar to its success as ideology or to its usefulness as propaganda to the elite. Nothing is more striking to Mosca and Pareto than the multiplicity of such ideologies in history allied with the regularity with which they have been used as a tool of the elite.

To the extent that the elite does consciously construct and propagate its ideological defence it is aided, the elitists argue, by its control of the communications media. The elitists accept Marx's assertion that "the ideas of the ruling class are, in every age, the ruling ideas". The dominant political class is at the same time the dominant intellectual class. Education, newspapers and the other mass media may all come under the control of the elite. Through these media the elite may spread the values and principles which implicitly legitimise the elite's position. In this the elite is aided, Wright Mills suggests, by the 'mass' character of the mass media. A single message is transmitted to millions of individuals in the mass, each of whom receives the message in isolation from the others. There is no scope for any response from the person in the mass. He cannot discuss or answer back. The flow of propaganda – possibly disguised as information – is one-way, from elite to mass. The members of the mass are receivers, not transmitters.[58]

By such techniques an elite can cultivate a legitimacy it might otherwise lack. According to Mosca and Pareto the mass is by no means averse to such social control. The mass, Mosca suggests, desires to be governed. It has no wish to take any political initiative. But the mass does not like to think of itself, or to be thought of, as succumbing to force. This would be an affront to human dignity. Political ideologies thus meet a real social need. They permit the mass to consider itself ruled according to some great moral principles. Pareto detects a certain idealism amongst the masses who are more likely to follow some grand principle such as nationalism than a calculation of self-interest which may be a more intricate matter to follow. Ideology, or 'derivation', thus satisfies the masses at the same time as controlling them.

THE PERPETUATION AND REPLACEMENT OF ELITES

Given the great accumulation of powers in the hands of an elite – economic wealth, governmental powers both legislative and bureaucratic, control over the means of communication – it may seem, at first sight, surprising that any elitist can speak of an elite as losing its dominant position. Yet just as Marx spoke of history as the history of class struggles, so Pareto spoke of it as the "graveyard of aristocracies".[59]

Elitists suggest two broad sets of factors to explain the downfall and replacement of elites – 'structural' factors and 'socio-psychological' factors. In the first case structural changes in the society bring about changes in the dominant minority in the society. The displacement of the elite occurs independently of the character and motivation of the elite. Burnham, following Marx in this point of his analysis, provides an instance of such an analysis. In the second case the elite is displaced as a result of some change in the attitudes or abilities of the elite. Mosca and Pareto represent, in their different ways, instances of this approach.

The Marxist has, by his own lights at least, a convincing explanation for social changes. According to Marx class change occurs as a consequence of a major change in the economic system which is itself caused by the introduction of new productive techniques to meet economic demands. As the new mode of production displaces the old economic forms so the class which is associated with the new means of production rises to dislodge the existing ruling class whose power is dependent on its ownership of the now outmoded productive forces. There is in Marx's view nothing of any substance that the existing ruling class can do to prevent the economic developments which result in its own overthrow. This incapacity to alter the course of history in an intended direction represents a very significant limitation to the power of Marx's ruling class. Marx repeatedly makes clear that these structural changes occur 'independently of the will' of the dominant class which by its own actions unconsciously digs its own grave. No amount of good resolutions or moral or political reform can alter the outcome. Marx is not, therefore, forced to suppose some decline in the capacity of the ruling class in order to explain its inability to control events from its apparently all-powerful position. In Burnham, too, the development of a contradiction between control of access to the means of production and control of preferential treatment in the distribution of the product which gives rise to a change in the ruling class is an inevitable process. Burnham, eclectic as ever, greatly dilutes this Marxian approach, however, by appearing to acknowledge that the degree of cohesion, consciousness and determination possessed by the elite may make some difference to the outcome.[60]

Mosca, by contrast, is less deterministic. There is, admittedly, something Marxian[61] about the way in which Mosca relates changes in elite domination to the rise of new interests or 'social forces' in a society. Where new economic interests develop or a new intellectual discovery is exploited or a new ideological movement wins allegiance the dominance of the elite is affected.[62] The composition of the elite, Mosca holds, will reflect the balance of social forces within the society. No ruling class can govern for long if it sets its face against the developments occurring in the society and the economy. Mosca's ruling class is not a veto group which can expect on all occasions to deny the implementation of policies for which all other groups in the society are pressing.[63] Rather the survival of the elite depends on its ability to adjust its own policies to meet the demands of the various interest groups. The elite aims, it appears, at a compromise which will satisfy the interests and yet leave the elite in its position of power. (To what extent an elite can continue to make concessions to the non-elite and still be said to 'rule' is an issue which Mosca fails to face. It will be discussed in a later chapter.)

Mosca's position however, differs fundamentally from that of Marx in two ways. Firstly, of course, the social forces which influence changes in the elite are much wider than the economic factors of Marx's analysis. Secondly, the ruling class is not helpless in the face of developments 'independent of its will'. Depending on its political skill and flexibility the elite may be able to ride out the storm and re-emerge in its dominant position. It may adapt its policies to meet the new pressures upon it but retain its original composition. More frequently, Mosca suggests, the ruling class will open its ranks – particularly the lower stratum – to the newer elements in society and so modify the composition of the class and the

interests it represents. This would not, however, be equivalent to a total class revolution. Rather, the new elements would be assimilated into the old ruling class.
The established elite would be renewed and invigorated by the ablest representatives of the new forces in the new society. At the same time the new elements in
turn become imbued with certain of the values of the elite. There is a fusion of elements rather than a total revolution. This process need not, moreover, be cataclysmic. The normal pattern of social mobility is for one group and then another,
one able individual and then another to enter the lower stratum of the elite in a
continuous process of 'molecular rejuvenation'. Cataclysmic change occurs as a
result of the ruling class being closed to recruitment from below – the denial of
the 'democratic tendency'. Such a closed elite results in a condition of 'class isolation' in which the rulers cease to be aware of fundamental currents of change in
society and hence lack the flexibility and skill to accommodate the new social
forces.

> Those who govern are unable to deal with the least flurry; and the changes
> that a strong and intelligent ruling class would have carried out at a negligi-
> ble cost in wealth, blood and human dignity take on the proportions of a social
> cataclysm.[64]

Cataclysms are not, it is clear, inevitable but are the consequence of avoidable
political mistakes on the part of the elite.

Pareto, as ever, is less easy to categorise. On the one hand the displacement of
one elite by another is as inevitable as any Marxian historical process. On the
other hand the change is explained in terms of the psychological make-up of the
elite and the non-elite rather than, as in Marx, in terms of some independent factor to which the elite necessarily reacts. The process of replacement occurs in two
ways by a gradual process of infiltration similar to that described by Mosca and
termed by Pareto the 'circulation of elites', or by a violent revolution involving
the total replacement of one elite by another. Pareto perceived a pattern in history
according to which there is a constant alternation between an elite with a prepon-
derance of Class I residues – the tender-minded 'foxes' – and an elite with a pre-
ponderance of Class II residues – the tough-minded 'lions'. The downfall of both
types of elite is explained in terms of psychological factors which ultimately inca-
pacitate both elites in their different ways for governing.

An elite of 'foxes' is marked by its political astuteness and ingenuity, its skill
in political manoeuvring – forming coalitions, rectifying party splits – its ability
to formulate policies to meet short-term needs or immediate crises. Its intellect is
displayed in the ideological justification it devises for its many political stances.
'Foxes', however, share the political vices which match their political virtues.
Force is, Pareto reminds us, as much a part of politics as is cunning and the
'foxes', filled with 'humanitarian' instincts inappropriate to politics, shrink from
its use. Their response to a problem which requires the short, sharp solution of
coercion is a further political manoeuvre. This tendency is endemic in such an

elite as 'foxes' recruit 'foxes' to the elite. It is pulled up short when the ineffectiveness of the regime brings about its violent overthrow at the hands of masses
led by a tough-minded (Class II residue) elite of 'lions' impatient to restore order
and strong government. But this new elite cannot last. Its vices, too, are the con-
comitants of its virtues. If cunning is by itself not enough in politics neither is
force and a respect for order. The tendency of an elite of 'lions' will be to become
too rigid and unresponsive to change. It lacks the imaginative qualities of the
'foxes'. As a result it either becomes too inflexible to withstand pressures – economic or military – from more imaginatively led states, or it fails to make economic and technical progress at home. Its only solution is to admit individuals
with Class I residues to enter the elite and remedy its intellectual and economic
deficiencies. By a steady process of upward social mobility the 'foxes' infiltrate
the elite until by Mosca's process of 'molecular rejuvenation' the elite is transformed into one of 'foxes'. The accession of the 'foxes' is, thus, a gradual one
whereas the 'lions' gain power by a sudden revolutionary uprising.

Figure 2

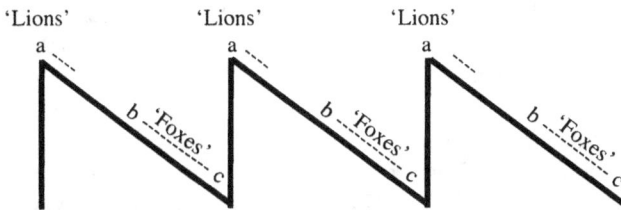

The process may be illustrated diagrammatically. In Figure 2 each peak represents the point at which the Class II elite has gained power and is at its 'purest'. It
is then infiltrated by 'foxes' (a-b) until the point is reached when it can be said that
the elite has been transformed into one of Class I residues (b-c).[65] The elite being
much smaller in numbers than the non-elite, it does not take a very large change
in the distribution of residues to transform the elite whilst the composition of the
mass remains extremely stable. The picture presented is, therefore, of a volatile
elite resting on a static society.

Associated with, but not identical to, the political cycle is an economic cycle.
Pareto makes a distinction between those persons ('rentiers') who live on fixed
incomes from rents, government bonds, life annuities, etc., and those ('speculators') whose income is variable and depends on their ingenuity in making profits.
'Rentiers' and 'speculators' are not politicians but are the economic element in the
governing class. They are not to be identified with 'lions' and 'foxes' although
'rentiers' share with the 'lions' a predominance of Class II residues and 'speculators', like 'foxes', are characterised by Class I residues. 'Rentiers' and 'speculators' are antagonistic in temperament and interests, the 'speculators' having most
to gain from inflationary situations which are the greatest danger to those on fixed
incomes. Moreover, the speculation is carried out with the savings of the rentiers.

There is an affinity between 'foxes' and 'speculators' in that both thrive on the same conditions. In 'pluto-democracies', in particular, the 'foxes' advantage lies in the ingenious political manoeuvre which will bring a speculator a quick profit.[66] At times the 'foxes' do appear to be the instruments of the 'speculators' as they might be in a Marxist analysis. But by and large the 'foxes' maintain their political dominance by a method of 'divide and rule' as they distribute favours to the various economic interests. The relation between 'lions' and 'rentiers' is less straightforward since the 'rentiers' may be exploited by a political elite with Class II residues ready to use force and supported by derivations which deceive the 'rentiers' into making sacrifices for the 'public interest'. On the other hand, 'rentiers' may well support revolutions of 'lions' against the association of 'foxes' and 'speculators'. Pareto is once again countering Marx by pointing out the frequency of middle class revolutions in history and implying that they would be a continuing phenomenon of political life – a claim supported by the experience of the twentieth century.

Though the political continuum is, in Pareto's view, one of the inevitable social laws this does not mean that a given elite is powerless to delay its operation. Class I elites are particularly unstable but even they may, with sufficient ingenuity, discover the one further manoeuvre that keeps them in power, or the more elaborate ideology (derivation) which convinces the mass of the need to support the status quo. Class II elites are intrinsically more stable and a regime based on military or police may stave off disaster for a considerable period – even centuries. Sparta represents a classic example of this. Regimes at an intermediate stage which have an elite with a mixture of Class I and Class II types may in particular survive for long periods before reverting to one or other of the 'pure' types. The "velocity of circulation" (§2043) gives a measure of how speedily the elite responds to changing conditions. This capacity of the elite to ensure that revolution will be very much later rather than sooner allows for a greater degree of independence and initiative for the political leadership than anything in Marx. The drawback here is a methodological one. Pareto's assertions about the inevitability of social change become in principle impossible to falsify and are hence less deserving of the term 'science'. No time limit to the duration of an elite is fixed. Even where an elite has survived for centuries Pareto can still claim that it is inherently unstable – it will degenerate 'in the long run'. That fewer elites do last this length of time is the result of the elite – which Pareto often conceives of as a loose coalition of leaders rather than a tightly-knit conspiratorial group – not acting with the maximum cohesion and decisiveness in the conscious defence of its interests.

The classical elitists' accounts of elite renewal, elite circulation or elite replacement were intended to illuminate what all thought to be the all-important underlying constancy – the existence in all social situations of a ruling minority and a ruled majority. The elitists see their accounts of social change as the very proof of their theories. The critic, however, might with equal justification conclude that these accounts are an attempt to save the consistency of the thesis of inevitable elite control in the face of the obvious social phenomenon of changes of rule.

NOTES

1   See the celebrated analysis by Karl Wittfogel, *Oriental Despotism*, Yale University Press, New Haven, 1957.

2   *Political Parties*, Free Press, Glencoe, 1915. (1958 reprinting cited), p. 423.

3   James H. Meisel, *The Myth of the Ruling Class: Gaetano Mosca and the Elite*, University of Michigan Press, Ann Arbor, 1958.

4   See below for a qualification of this in respect of Pareto.

5   *Leviathan*, Ch. 10.

6   *The Ruling Class*, McGraw-Hill, New York, 1939. Ch. XV §3, p. 404.

7   Mosca, *The Ruling Class*, XV, §3, p. 410.

8   *The Power Elite*, Oxford University Press, New York, 1956. Galaxy Book edition, 1959, cited, pp. 288–90.

9   *The Machiavellians*, John Day, New York, 1943; Gateway, Chicago, 1963.

10 *The Ruling Class*, Ch. II, §I; McGraw-Hill 1939 edition, p. 50.

11 See, for example, Ch. I, §I6, p. 39.

12 *The Ruling Class*, Ch. II, §3, p. 53.

13 *The Ruling Class*, Ch. II, §3, p. 53.

14 Mosca's discussion of this point is mainly in the earlier work *Teorica dei governi e governo Parlamentare* and is treated extensively by Meisel, *The Myth of the Ruling Class*.

15 *The Ruling Class*, Ch. VI, §I, p. 154.

16 Quoted by Meisel, *The Myth of the Ruling Class*, p. 106.

17 The English text entitled *The Ruling Class* is a conflation of two volumes of Mosca's *Elementi di scienza politica*, the first volume of which appeared in 1896 and the second in 1923. The second volume (Chs. 12–17 of *The Ruling Class*) represents a considerable shift in Mosca's position, especially as regards representative democracy. The still earlier *Teorica dei governi e governo Parlamentare* (1884) criticised representative government even more severely.

18 See *The Ruling Class*, Ch. XV.

19 These points are discussed further below under the heading 'Perpetuation and replacement of elites'.

20 *The Ruling Class*, Ch. XV, §7, p. 429.

21 *The Ruling Class*, Ch. XIV, §8, p. 389.

22 *The Ruling Class*, Ch. XVII, §6, p. 493.

23 *The Ruling Class*, Ch. XV, §4, p. 413.

24 *The Ruling Class*, Ch, XVII, §6, p. 492.

25 *Political Parties*, Free Press, 1958 reprint; p. 418.

26 See the elaborate analysis by C. W. Cassinelli, 'The Law of Oligarchy', *American Political Science Review*, Vol. 47, No.3, 1953, pp. 773–84.

27 *Political Parties*, pp. 288–9.

28 *Political Parties*, Part I, Sec. B, Ch. II.

29 *The Ruling Class*, pp. 422 ff.

30 On Michels's attitude to democracy, see J. D. May, 'Democracy, Organization, Michels', *American Political Science Review*, LIX, 2, June, 1965, pp, 417–29. Mays's interpretation

of Michels differs in essential respects from that offered here.

31 S. E. Finer, *Vilfredo Pareto: Sociological Writings*, p. 77.

32 *Sociological Writings*, p. 248 (§2027).

33 *Sociological Writings*, p, 248 (§2031).

34 *The Mind and Society*, §§1858, 2191, 2480.

35 See below.

36 *Sociological Writings*, pp. 268–9 (§2254).

37 For further discussion see S. E. Finer, *Vilfredo Pareto: Sociological Writings*, pp. 72–77.

38 *The Managerial Revolution*, Putnam, London, 1942; p. 56.

39 *The Managerial Revolution*, p. 57.

40 Burnham's account of class revolution will be discussed below along with other theories of the circulation of elites.

41 Such an analysis had first been suggested in Thorstein Veblen's celebrated *The Theory of the Leisure Class* in 1899.

42 *The Power Elite*, Oxford University Press, Galaxy edition, 1959; p. 4.

43 *The Power Elite*, p. 19.

44 *The Power Elite*, p. 288.

45 Cp. R. Aron, 'Social Structure and the Ruling Class', *British Journal of Sociology*, Vol. I, No. 1–2 (1950), pp. 1–16 and 126–43.

46 *The Power Elite*, pp. 15, 19.

47 *The Power Elite*, pp. 278–80.

48 *The Power Elite*, p. 4.

49 *The Power Elite*, pp. 20 ff; *The Sociological Imagination*, Oxford University Press, New York, 1959; Evergreen edition, New York, 1961, pp. 181–2.

50 *The Power Elite*, pp. 20–5; *The Sociological Imagination*, p. 40.

51 *The Power Elite*, p. 7.

52 *The Sociological Imagination*, p. 182.

53 *The Power Elite*, pp. 321 ff.

54 *The Power Elite*, p. 322.

55 *What is to be done? Passim.*

56 Mosca, *The Ruling Class*, II, §3, p. 53.

57 See *The Ruling Class*, III, §I, pp. 70–1.

58 Mills, *The Power Elite*, Ch. 13.

59 *Sociological Writings*, p. 249 (§2053).

60 *The Managerial Revolution*, p. 63.

61 See Meisel, *The Myth of the Ruling Class*, p. 303; T. Bottomore, *Elites and Society*, Watts, London, 1964, pp. 26–7, 50–1.

62 *The Ruling Class*, II, §8, pp. 65–9.

63 Cp. Dahl's criteria for a 'ruling elite'.

64 *The Ruling Class*, IV, §6, p. 119.

65 Pareto makes some reference to a counter-cycle whereby a Class I elite is infiltrated by men of Class II residues who finally become dominant and close off the elite to those with Class I residues. Pareto does not, however develop this.

66 See, e.g., §§2254–6, 2454, 2480–4.

chapter three | elitism and pluralism

One major theme of political and social analysis since the late nineteenth century has been the view that there has been a tendency for the directive power in modern society to be concentrated in fewer and fewer hands. This opinion won both academic and popular favour again in the 1950s in both Britain and America. In Britain the term 'the establishment' became a catchphrase of political journalism and television pundits. Allegations of a 'leak' of an intended change in Bank Rate led to a public inquiry, to newspaper speculation and comment and to academic investigation of the connections – social, political and economic – on 'top decision-makers'.[1] In the USA, C. Wright Mills's *Power Elite* excited academic controversy and popular interest and gained for its author a strong following amongst radicals on both sides of the Atlantic. One of its major claims obtained support from an unexpected quarter in President Eisenhower's farewell address to the American people in 1957 in which he warned them of the influence of the "military-industrial complex" in "every city, every State House, every office of the Federal Government". To the elitist such a tendency cannot be regarded as novel. It is instead a truth of human history that power is always concentrated, though the manner of the concentration can vary from period to period. The essential characteristic of 'the establishment' was the survival into the mid-twentieth century of what Cobbett called 'The Thing' and Marx 'Old England'. The popular appeal of such elitist suggestions frequently reflects the persistent fascination with 'conspiracy theories' of society which offer explanations – however implausible at times – of what their advocates regard as the abuses of power and which, equally importantly, identify a culprit or discover a scapegoat.[2] But this belief in the tendency for power to be concentrated and cumulative has not gone unchallenged. Throughout the same period of the development of modern politics this analysis has faced a converse thesis which claims that power in modern society has tended to become diffused. The argument runs somewhat as follows.[3] The history of 'advanced' societies such as those of Western Europe or the USA is one of a transition from a simple, homogenous form of society to a complex, differentiated form. The more primitive the society the smaller the range of human activities it comprises. Its economy is geared only to primary production. Its instruments of production are few. Social unity is reinforced by common traditions embracing religion, morality, law and 'politics'– activities not on this view strictly separable in such integrated communities. In such a society a man may play many parts not merely in his lifetime but concurrently. Specialisation has not yet made it too difficult to acquire new skills or to switch activities as need arises – from, for instance, farmer to warrior. Leadership is similarly unspecialised with judicial, rule-making, executive and priestly powers in the same hands.

Society becomes more differentiated with division of labour. Secondary industries and ultimately tertiary services supplement the old primary-producing economy. Men increasingly become specialists in their own particular activities. As specialism increases it becomes more difficult for individuals to undertake new activities without undergoing new training, and it is rarer for one man to play a number of roles at anyone time. Each new major trade or industry in a society providing new occupations, altering the property relationships and introducing new sources of wealth will make an impact on the society's power structure. Ultimately, this thesis continues, each new development's existence and interests will need to be recognised and accommodated by a change in the ruling personnel or else by some alteration in policy.

Those performing an activity thus tend to convert themselves into an 'interest group' to exert pressure on the ruling bodies in the society. This was recognised by Mosca in his discussion of the need of the ruling class to acknowledge and respond to the major 'social forces' which press on the elite from below. In the USA the analysis of politics in terms of the inter-play of interest groups became a major branch of political science, whose leading practitioners were A. F. Bentley (*The Process of Government*, 1908) and David Truman (*The Governmental Process*, 1951). Their analysis is essentially pluralistic. The political game is played by a great variety of groups each seeking some advantage to itself. Government is the focal point for group pressure and its task is to effect a policy which reflects the highest common factor of group demands. According to this argument, in such pluralistic, differentiated societies the management of public affairs tends to be shared between a number of persons and bodies, frequently differing in their values, the sources and methods of their recruitment and their methods of wielding influence. Often they are rivals for influence over society at large.

Moreover, the process of diversification is a continuing one. Significantly, Robert A. Dahl entitles the first, historical, section of *Who Governs?*[4], his classic study of New Haven politics, 'From Oligarchy to Pluralism'. He describes the simple urban community of New Haven before the 1840s and then traces the diversification of its society and economy with the advent of industry and business and of a working class of varied ethnic origin. The resultant situation, as Dahl describes it, is that no one power group is able to control the community. Instead, a number of rival leaders compete for power by each attempting to construct loose coalitions from the local interest groups so as to form a majority to secure election to office. Thus power has been dispersed in response to the diversification of interest groups and 'political resources', as Dahl terms the votes, the jobs, the threats, the money, the information which enable one person to influence the political behaviour of another. A similar contrast between a less 'developed', unified power structure and a modern diversified one is drawn by Robert E. Scott in a discussion of political elites and political modernisation in Latin America.[5] Scott suggests that the more traditional Latin American societies are still dominated by a unified power elite[6] of large landowners, army and Church, whilst those societies which have undergone the experience of modernisation contain a multiplicity of interests and elites. Even these societies, however, have not attained the degree of elite specialisation which Scott finds in the USA or the more advanced countries of Western Europe. In particular they lack a strong elite of professional politicians with firm bases in parties and legislatures who can arbitrate between and coordinate the various competing elites. Instead, the specialised elites intervene, whether in a legal or extra-legal fashion, directly in the political arena rather than exert pressure upon the political decision making process.

These pluralistic analyses of the power structure offer a picture of diversity but not of equality. They deny that modern societies are under the control of a single elite but they do not claim that such societies are egalitarian. Some groups have more influence on social affairs than others, but the several groups do not coalesce. In Dahl's terms inequality in the distribution of 'political resources' does not imply the existence of one ruling elite. Moreover, the 'pluralists' acknowledge that within each interest group or within any specialised activity there will tend to be an inner core of leaders or of the most active participants.

Allen Potter has divided organised interest groups into two main types – 'spokesman groups' which represent and defend established sectional interests such as trades unions or ex-servicemen, and 'promotional groups' which foster causes and organise people who share a particular attitude to an issue such as nature conservancy or civil liberties.[7] Potter discovered that spokesman groups, however democratic and representative in their formal organisation, rapidly developed into oligarchies. Power to negotiate tends to be concentrated in few hands.[8] Promotional groups are simply 'natural' oligarchies in that they are less formally organised and tend to be led by those most actively interested in the particular cause, who also have the time to spare and can afford to take on what is often unpaid or poorly paid work.[9] In either case the groups display the typical oligarchical pyramid with a very few leaders and a wide base of those with little influence on group policy.

Whereas the 'classical' elitists see the social structure as analogous in shape to a single pyramid, the 'pluralist-elitists' see it as a range of pyramids. Dahl hypothesises that in modern democracies different sets of persons will be prominently involved in each particular area of policy-making. Leaders will, in general, be specialists in one 'issue-area' as Dahl terms it. The minority which is influential in issues concerning defence will not be the same minority as determines housing policy or as sits around the negotiating table to settle a labour dispute. Dahl sought to isolate three such issue areas in his study of New Haven – the making of party nominations for local elective offices, public education and urban renewal. He concluded that there was virtually no overlap of membership between the minorities involved in each of the issue areas. Only the elected mayor was involved in all three issues, and only one other person – a leader in the urban redevelopment programme – made any contribution to decisions outside his own specialism.[10] This is not to say that the several minorities existed in total isolation from one another.[11] But Dahl found no signs of a single elite operating behind the scenes to coordinate the policies of public officials and impose its will on community affairs.

The argument of pluralists such as Dahl is, then, that in advanced democratic societies political decisions will tend to be influenced by a number of elites. The term 'elite', if used at all by such theorists, is used in a weakened sense to mean merely the category of 'top persons' in any interest group or in any activity which affects politics. In this sense it is akin to Pareto's first formal definition of an elite[12] but without the implication that those 'at the top' are necessarily the most able members of the group. In a world of imperfect political competition they may have birth or wealth on their side, or may just have been lucky.

TYPES OF ELITE

On this understanding of elite there could be as many elites as there are activities in which a number of human beings indulge. It is obvious, however, that not all such elites will play an important part in political affairs. We may, then, adapt Pareto and speak of political elites and non-political elites. It assists categorisation, however, if we refer to 'elites in politics' and confine 'political elite' to the elite of politicians themselves.

Many attempts have been made to classify such elites or to isolate those which have the greatest political significance. Elites may in the first place be seen in relation to some wider classification of structures of influence. The most common such classification made by political scientists and sociologists is the distinction between the hierarchies of power, wealth (or, not entirely the same thing, class) and status. These three dimensions are in principle separable even if the distinctions present some problems for empirical investigation. The exercise of 'power', in this context, refers to one's ability to participate effectively in decisions which substantially alter the balance of advantages and disadvantages of courses of action open to others. The decisions may be governmental or administrative or they may be taken in the factory or office. The concept of power is a very intricate one which admits of a number of further distinctions, one of which may be noted here. There is a legal power – more properly legal 'authority' – and there is a *de facto* power. Situations often arise, particularly in revolutionary periods, when the legal political authority lacks the ability to make and enforce laws whilst effective power lies with a 'power behind the throne' such as a military *junta*. In principle it might seem possible to arrange persons and groups in a hierarchy with those with greatest power in a specific area of decision-making at the top, and those with least power at the base. But it is not necessarily true that there is a single such hierarchy of power for the whole of a society since a person's or a group's power is very often confined to only one area of decisionmaking.[13]

The hierarchy of wealth is much more straightforward. Those with the largest income and the greatest accumulation of capital would constitute the elite of wealth. Class is a more complicated matter. A person's class is, according to most definitions, determined by the position he occupies along with others in relation to the productive process. Marx's chief distinction was between the class which owned and the class which operated the means of production. But classes may be further distinguished by the amount and form (wages, salaries, fees) of payment, degree of job security, amount of unemployment benefit and retirement pension, and the range and type of other 'fringe benefits' and 'perks'. Though some of these differentials may be the outcome of the exercise of political power – by means of pensions legislation, for instance – they derive for the large part from the division of labour established by the prevailing productive process. Economic classes may then also be arranged hierarchically according to the number and range of 'life chances' possessed by their respective members. 'Life chances' refers here to the economic resources described earlier and, indeed, to opportunities for education, for acquiring culture or for enjoying good health. These opportunities are related in the first place to economic position even though they may be affected favourably or unfavourably by the exercise of political power.

Status, the last of this trio of dimensions, depends upon social opinion. A person has high status in a society when either he or the group or activity with which he is associated is valued highly by the rest of the community. He may gain personal status by performing some outstanding action, but here we are more concerned with status which attaches to groups. Engineers, scientists, doctors may all have high status in certain societies because of their contribution to social welfare and prosperity. In other societies membership of a particular race or religion gives prestige, in still others it is attendance at a certain school, or birth into a celebrated family. According to Max Weber, from whom modern sociological analysis of status derives,[14] each 'status group' will possess its own 'style of life' which distinguishes it from other such groups. This 'style of life' embraces dress, recreation, membership of clubs or church. The difference between the 'class' and 'status' dimensions is summarised by Weber:

> With some over simplification, one might thus say that 'classes' are stratified according to their relations to the production and acquisition of goods; whereas 'status groups' are stratified according to the principles of their consumption of goods as represented by special 'styles of life'.[15]

Status groups seek, Weber suggests, to make themselves and their style of life more exclusive. They thereby promote social 'distance' between themselves and other groups. At the same time each group aims to secure a privileged social position for itself. In some cases groups are able to obtain legal and institutional recognition for their status privileges. The sumptuary laws of many countries awarded in the past privileges of dress to specific groups. Nowadays, in certain countries, including the UK, many professions, particularly law and medicine, are permitted by law to control entry by setting their own examinations for qualification and to impose rules and sanctions to secure 'ethical' conduct. The ideal situation for any status group is to be in habitual receipt of such widespread deference to its style of life that it can thereby obtain a dominant economic and political position. This, according to Weber, was the way of priestly status groups. The religion begins as a 'style of life' of a small group of prophets and ends as the ethos of a whole civilisation. At the same time the religion grants a dominating position to its professional upholders. This domination then often extends, as in medieval Europe, into the society and the economy.

Once again one might arrange the many status groups in a society in a hierarchy of prestige taking the status elite to be the group whose style of life is most widely esteemed. There is, however, no reason to suppose that there will be a single hierarchy of status in any given society any more than there will necessarily be a single hierarchy of power.[16] A group's prestige, like a group's power, may be largely confined to one realm of activity. A particular football club may rank high in a table of sporting prestige but carry little or no weight outside the world of sport. To gain true elite status there must either be a generally accepted ranking of the activities themselves – politics, business, religion, fashion, sport – or else a group must carry its prestige over into a number of fields. An example might be an aristocracy which occupies public and religious office, sets fashions and wins prestige in suitably gentlemanly sports.

We have seen that the elitist regards power as cumulative. For him power, wealth and status generally go together. Wealth and status are in fact forms of power. The pluralist, by contrast, argues that the three are by no means necessarily conjoined and that in fact they are often found apart. Dahl's New Haven study again furnishes evidence on this score. He carefully distinguishes between the 'social notables' and 'economic notables' and he finds scarcely any overlap between the two groups or between either group and the holders of political power. Certainly the view that there is any necessary connection between the possession of these three 'goods' is false.[17] It is frequently the case, particularly in tradition-minded societies, that wealth, especially new wealth, does not automatically confer elite status. Equally political power, particularly in modern democracies with strong working-class parties, does not inevitably go to those with greatest wealth or the highest social standing. Elites of wealth, power and status may, moreover, be antagonistic. A long-established status group may well find that its interests clash with those of the wealthy. One of the prime functions of political power in modern times has been to restrict the advantages of the wealthy by such measures as redistributive taxation, nationalisation of industry and trust-busting legislation.

On the other hand the pluralist emphasis on the need to distinguish elites of power, wealth and status may lead to an over-compartmentalisation which is methodologically misleading.[18] Weber, in making the original distinction, pointed out that the style of life enjoyed by a privileged status group must be conditioned by its economic circumstances.[19] Though in principle distinct from classes many, but not all, status groups are recruited from within a single class and do not straddle class boundaries. At the same time the exercise of power, particularly in the making of decisions in business and industry, has been closely connected with the ownership of economic resources. The pluralist can therefore refute any elitist assertion of the necessary concentration of power, wealth and status in the hands of one elite. Whether these advantages are dispersed between three sets of leaders, as Dahl discovered to be the case in New Haven, must, however, await investigation in each particular instance.

S. F. Nadel offers a different categorisation of elites[20] which at least serves as a useful guide through a wealth of empirical material. He distinguishes three types of elite – 'social elites', 'specialised elites' and 'governing elites'. 'Social elites' and 'specialised elites' are both forms of status group. The influence a social elite exerts is indirect. It does not command deference by virtue of its coercive power or any 'monopoly of decision-making'. Its influence arises, Nadel argues, simply because it is looked up to and is imitated by other groups in the society. Its imitable qualities may range from table manners and accent to cultural or sporting interests. There may be one such model elite in a community whose style of life is copied by those who aim to 'get on' socially, or there could be several such elites each having qualities thought worthy of imitation.

Nadel's 'governing elite' is composed of the society's political rulers. He assumes it to have a 'decisive pre-eminence' over other elites rather than to be merely one elite amongst others. Its pre-eminence derives from its legislative and coercive authority over the most general affairs of the community. The scope of its influence, Nadel implies, is so much wider than that of any other elite as to make it an elite different in kind from any other. A Marxist would, of course, find this definition tendentious in that it presupposes the fundamental importance of politics rather than economics as the key to the structure of power in a community. It may, of course, be true in particular cases that a political elite holds 'decisive pre-eminence' in a society. In a recent study of the relationship between British politics and society Jean Blondel concluded that the politicians did possess this decisive position:

> The return of one party to power rather than that of the other, sets the tone of political life. It determines, not so much what the cards are, but what each hand is going to be. Interest groups may have many of the good cards, they are not the ones who shuffle them.[21]

Even so, this pre-eminence may only be won by a great deal of bargaining involving considerable concessions to the interest groups. Formal constitutional arrangements may also decisively affect the power wielded by the politicians and, indeed, raise the issue as to whether 'the politicians' comprise a unified group. A federal system such as that of the USA considerably restricts the government's freedom of action. Budget plans, foreign commitments, welfare programmes desired by a President are commonly rejected by the legislature. Bargaining,[22] endemic to most pluralist democracies, is built into a federal system.

Politicians do not, however, necessarily possess this pre-eminence. They may be the agents of the interest groups, as Robert E. Scott suggests they are in Latin America.[23] They may even be the executive arm of the ruling class, as the Marxists would have it: "The Cabinet and its Committees...may be said to represent the main forums...where finance capital can decide State policy".[24]

In estimating the influence of the political leadership it is also necessary to take into account the strength of the political institutions themselves. One must look at the prestige of the legislature amongst the population and at the capacity of the assembly or the cabinet to oversee and integrate the departments of state, and the public and private sectors of the economy. Doubts have been frequently expressed on this point in Britain, which may claim to possess one of the most authoritative sets of political institutions. Parliament, it is said, has insufficient time and staff and inadequate machinery to carry out its basic task of acting as the 'grand inquest of the nation' by criticising and publicising government measures, and enquiring into administrative efficiency and justice. Ministers no longer even claim to know everything that is carried out in their name by their departments. The Cabinet cannot determine the whole range of social and economic policy. There has, consequently, been a distinct tendency to place crucial areas of the economy under the direction of semi-independent bodies rather than under strict ministerial control. The nationalised industries are run by public corporations rather than as departments of state, and have a considerable degree of autonomy in determining policy and a considerable degree of independence in day-to-day administration. Hence arose the paradox whereby the British Government's economic policy of a 'pay pause' could receive its first damaging defeat in 1959 at the hands of the directors of the state-owned electricity industry.

The degree of autonomy possessed by the elite is thus one of the central factors in explaining its power structure. For many writers, Raymond Aron[25] and Robert A. Dahl[26] are particularly clear on this; the degree of autonomy possessed by the elites of a society is a measure of democracy. A democracy, as opposed to a totalitarian regime, is distinguished by the larger degree of independence enjoyed by the pressure groups, parties, unions, churches and the rest. A totalitarian system tends to make every group or 'sub-system' an arm of the regime. Each group is integrated with the government by means of central officials or by the dominant party and its agents. Even within a pluralistic democracy the extent of such autonomy can vary. The one extreme occurs where a group is granted the right by law to regulate its own affairs, controlling entry and maintaining its own standards, allowing few powers to appeal from its decisions to an outside body or set of rules. Closer to the other extreme is where a group acts in a surrogate capacity for the government, its continuing freedom of movement depending largely on its satisfying the government's desires. The current (1968) wage-vetting activities of the Trades Union Congress in Britain approaches such a situation. The degree of autonomy possessed by the boards of British nationalised industries has already been mentioned and can range from the considerable autonomy of the BBC to the frequent governmental interventions in the policy-making of the nationalised airlines. The governing elite may itself be a social elite, as in some aristocratic regimes where the rulers hold themselves up as models of social behaviour. Castiglione's *The Book of the Courtier* is a celebrated handbook for Renaissance governing circles, reminding them of their role as a social elite. A governing elite may utilise the prestige of the 'social elites' to facilitate acceptance of its policy by, for instance, obtaining the support of intellectuals, fashion idols or 'pop stars'. On the other hand, it may be hostile to the ideals of the social elites – puritanical, anti-intellectual or suspicious of the social prestige of a traditional upper-class.

'Specialised elites', Nadel's final category, are the eminent groups of their own particular professions, trades or activities. This is again the weakened sense of the term referred to earlier, though Nadel then adds that such groups must also show a degree of corporateness and exclusiveness to count as an elite rather than a mere category. The specialised political elite might be the party leaders or the Parliamentary ministers. The specialised union elite might be the elected national leadership or even in some circumstances the elected shop stewards. Some of these specialised elites might also be 'social elites'. This will not be a consequence of their own specialised skills but will result from what Nadel calls 'spill-over' qualities – certain standards or ideals which they share and which may be thought worthy of imitation by the rest of society. The specialised skill of the scientific elite, for instance, could not be imitated by the general public, but the ideals of the research scientist – 'objectivity', dedication to furthering knowledge – may be esteemed, publicised and imitated, particularly in a technocratically-minded society. There may also be an overlap between a specialised elite and the governing elite. One instance, frequent enough in recent years, is the military regime.

These specialised elites again could, in principle, be as many and varied as there are human activities. Not all such elites, however, are politically significant and it seems advisable to distinguish a sub-group amongst the specialised elites of those which exercise a substantial degree of influence on the policies of the governing elite or of other specialised elites. These are the elites with which the governing elite must bargain, and to which it may have to defer. They include amongst others the business elite whose investment decisions and 'confidence' substantially influence a governing elite's economic and social-welfare programme; the union elite whose strike decision affects a nation's balance of payments situation; the military elite whose degree of commitment to civilian rule is a crucial factor, as modern experience reminds us, in determining the survival of the governing elite; the religious elite whose blessing and cooperation was, particularly in past eras, essential to securing the legitimacy of the civil order. No one generally accepted name designates these influential elites although Suzanne Keller has coined the handy label 'strategic elite'.[27]

A large number of studies of 'specialised' or 'strategic' elites have been published in recent years. The approaches adopted have been very varied both as to method and intention. Many of the studies have been confined to a particular elite in one country – Kelsall on the British civil service,[28] Wright Mills on the union elite in the USA,[29] Armstrong on the Soviet bureaucracy.[30] Comparative studies have been rarer in large part because of the financial costs of such research. Some of the methodological issues will be discussed in the following chapters. The remainder of this chapter will be devoted to indicating, by reference to a few widely discussed topics, some of the lines that elite research has followed in recent years. Works on the military, business, bureaucracy, education and the 'establishment' will be taken to suggest the range of current interest in elites.

MILITARY ELITES

Military elites have been studied historically for their impact on the politics of a society. An outstanding example is Gordon A. Craig's study of *The Politics of the Prussian Army*[31], which traces the ebb and flow of army influence on the domestic and foreign policy of Prussia and Germany from the seventeenth to the twentieth century. Craig demonstrates the army's role in the creation of the state, the strength and limitations of its position in the caste-like structure of Frederick the Great's Prussia, its brief period as a reforming institution and 'school for the nation' in the years of post-Napoleonic recovery, its reversion to a conservative, anti-democratic standpoint and its, in part, self-defeating step of accepting Hitler in order to escape the constitutional restraints of democracy.

The study has more than a parochial interest for students of German history. It examines factors important to many elite studies – the military elite's class background, the socialisation process it undergoes, the nature of its values, and the extent to which these elements make for a cohesive, conscious and 'conspiratorial' leadership group. It illuminates the potential influence of a military elite where a society's political traditions have not firmly established the respective roles of the civil and the military leadership. Finally, it traces the all-important steps – frequently omitted in elite studies[32] – by which potential power is translated into actual power in policy formation and political action.

Other approaches to military elites can illustrate alternative aspirations not merely for elite analysis but for social science in general. S.E. Finer[33] examines many of the same factors as does Craig – educational background, social origins, belief in the legitimacy of the political regime, character of civil-military relations – but he casts his net wider to take in a range of societies. His approach, though using historical data, is less historical in intention and the aim is to establish not the dynamics of one particular military elite but to outline a typology of military elites and their political potentialities on which to base comparative analysis. Finer's book also provides an introduction to the literature on military elites in developing countries which has, understandably, grown at an enormous rate in the 1960s. The sociological is combined with the historical approach in Morris Janowitz's *The Professional Soldier*.[34] This 'social and political portrait' examines the formative influence of the political culture and related professional values upon the structure of the military service and the attitudes of the soldier. Concentrating on the development of the American military elite in this century, Janowitz explores many of the main themes of elitist discussion such as the extent to which elite consciousness breeds consciousness and the growing significance of organisational and managerial skills.

BUSINESS ELITES

The major concern of both American and British studies of the elites of industry and business has been to examine the contention, made popular, as we have seen, by James Burnham, that a new elite of managers is rapidly displacing the capitalist class as the source of economic decision-making. Burnham, of course, claimed more than that the managers would constitute a significant specialised or strategic elite. The managers were to form a new ruling elite exercising political and administrative as well as economic domination. The more recent empirical investigations, however, have been largely confined to establishing the managers' role in the economic realm. Evidence of the growing importance of the manager is readily available from academic sources such as the pioneering study by A. A. Berle and G. C. Means, *The Modern Corporation and Private Property*[35] or P. Sargent Florence's detailed analysis *Ownership, Control and Success of Large Companies*[36] as well as from the many news stories and feature articles in the national press.

On the one side is the argument that the vast scale of modern corporations has meant that shareholding is very widely dispersed. To own even a 1 per cent share in a giant company such as Shell is almost beyond the means of the wealthiest of individuals. Instead, the wealthy spread their investments amongst a large number of companies. Shareholding is fragmented. In many companies the vast majority of shareholders own fewer than 500 shares each. Each individual shareholder, the argument goes, is too weak to exercise any major policy influence whilst the total number of shareholders is too large for effective coordinated action. In this power vacuum the managers are able to take the major decisions with only the most formal reference to the annual meeting of shareholders. In Britain the top managers frequently hold seats on the boards of directors but they rarely hold a significant proportion of company shares. Where managers are not directors they are even less likely to be shareholders. Moreover, the larger the company the fewer instances of large shareholding by manager-directors.[37] From this evidence of the 'divorce of ownership from control' the conclusion is drawn that the managers are an elite with interests which radically diverge from those of the capitalists. Whilst the shareholders wish to see profits used to increase short-term dividends, the managers are interested in long-term stability and the maintenance of the corporate organisation and for these reasons want profits to be ploughed back into the firm.

The counter-argument is two-fold – that the capitalists are still in control and that the managers do not radically differ in background, interests or outlook from the capitalists. Two main pieces of evidence may be adduced to substantiate the claim that the capitalists still exercise power over industry. Firstly, Florence's study of English companies showed that personal owner-control was more frequent even amongst large companies than had been believed. Moreover, Florence's test for such control – 20 per cent of the voting shares – is an extremely severe one, given that experience has shown that a holding of only 6 per cent can be decisive in determining a firm's policy where the remaining holdings are extremely fragmented. A less severe test would probably have revealed a larger number of personally owned and controlled companies. On the other hand Florence also found that beyond a certain size ownership is beyond the means of anyone man or family.[38]

Secondly, it is often asserted that capitalist control is maintained through a system of 'interlocking directorships' which reflects the investment of one firm in another and, especially, the large institutional investments by banks, insurance companies and nominees. These interlocking directors would form the inner core of the industrial elite. The great network of controlling and subsidiary companies, holding companies and trusts so typical of modern industrial societies certainly indicates a greater concentration of control than would appear from the number of listed companies. Not all interlocking directorships, however, represent this pattern of control. Many individuals who sit on several boards are called in for advice and contacts rather than as executive directors. Others, in Britain at least, are thought to bring prestige to the company, particularly if they possess titles. These multiple directors may help promote a sense of common interest amongst the company directorates but the picture of a few hundred men making concerted policy decisions on a vast number of independent companies is almost certainly false. Executive directors tend to be confined to one company and many of the largest British companies have no directors with seats on the boards of other companies.[39]

The claim that interlocking directorships between industrial companies and banks indicate that industry is controlled by the bankers[40] is also open to question when the British evidence is examined. That such directorships-in-common exist cannot, of course, be disputed. What is at issue is their significance. Are the directors to be considered the representatives of banking capital controlling the industrial boards of the country? Or is it rather the case, as so many of the examples documented by Barratt-Brown suggest, that the managerial elite of industry often finds it convenient for the sake of financial advice and business contacts to take up seats on the boards of the major financial institutions?[41] It seems a reasonable surmise that many of the professional bankers who sit on the boards of industry are there to keep a watching brief for the shareholders they represent as nominees or to offer counsel on financial matters. Many of the largest firms in Britain have no directors in common with financial institutions whilst the very largest companies can be financially independent of the banks. Smaller, expanding firms tend to be more dependent on outside financial support.[42]

More striking than any control by the financiers over industry is the potential conflict between the industrialists and managers on the one hand, interested in easy credit in order to expand, and the banking elite on the other, for whom high interest rates and the stability of the currency can mean high profits. Marx noted such a conflict between the industrial faction and the financial faction of the bourgeoisie in the France of Louis Philippe.[43] More recently there is strong evidence that the revived interest in economic planning in Britain in the 1960s owed much to the opposition of leading industrialists and managers to the alleged influence of the City of London and the Treasury on the deflationary economic policies followed by the government.[44]

A more persuasive argument against the theory of a growing conflict of interests between owners and managers of industry is that the background, career and outlook of the managerial elite in Western capitalist or mixed economies are in no fundamental way different from those of the capitalists. C. Wright Mills has stressed the dependence of the managers on the profitability of private enterprise for their high salaries, expense accounts, company-financed holidays and company-backed scholarships for their children.[45] Managers tend to have spent their entire careers in one or other aspect of private enterprise and to be as fully committed to its maintenance as the owners of capital themselves. A number of studies of managers in the USA and the UK have also shown that in the past managers have been heavily recruited from the same wealthier classes as have produced the capitalist entrepreneurs.[46]

Most observers would appear to agree with Florence that there has been "a managerial evolution if not a revolution".[47] It is much less certain however, that this development has radically altered the nature of capitalism. An examination of the business elite does, however, serve as an illustration of something that can be true of many other specialised elites – that they are not monolithic groups but may themselves be composed of sub-groups (elites) which differ in interests and in outlook. Thus managers may have to be distinguished not only from owners of capital but from financiers and also – as Burnham failed to do – managers of big businesses need to be distinguished from managers of medium and small businesses. Even then there may be major differences of views such as have occurred in Britain in recent years among those in each category. On the one hand there are those top managers who reaffirm the desirability of free competition and independence from government control and on the other those who support governmental attempts at forward planning and rationalisation of industry even to the extent of accepting administrative posts.

BUREAUCRATIC ELITES

Some of the earliest fears of elite domination were prompted by the growth of bureaucracy in central government, in the political parties, the unions and even in industry. James Burnham saw bureaucratic dominance as an aspect of managerial control. This contention, along with the issues raised by Max Weber's classic analysis,[48] have been the main problems discussed in studies of bureaucracy as a specialised elite. Burnham predicted that the distinction made by liberal theory between state and economy would increasingly break down as the state found it more and more necessary to intervene in the economy whether through nationalisation, government subsidies or economic planning. One result would be that the jobs of government administrator and business manager would become more alike. The same skills and training would be needed and the two roles would be readily interchangeable. At the same time the Weberian analysis suggested that the bureaucracy could very easily obtain a dominant position by means of its organisation of information and the efficiency of its executive hierarchy unless it were balanced by a powerful body of responsible elected political leaders. The ideal politician, Weber suggested, was the man of principle and action. The ideal official was the man prepared to execute conscientiously and efficiently whatever his political superiors legislated, regardless of his own private convictions.[49] But where such strong political leadership is lacking or where there has been no long tradition of political activity officialdom may overstep its bounds and take on the direction of affairs. The administrative elite is then more than a specialised elite and becomes the *de facto* ruling group.

Civil service rule has frequently been alleged to prevail in France since the war. France has traditionally possessed a strong centralised officialdom, and in the face of the succession of weak governments during the Fourth Republic the bureaucracy increasingly took the initiative, particularly in restoring the economy. Officials of the French planning machinery give directions backed by sanctions on matters such as the location of industry, which in Britain, for instance, would have considerable political implications and would consequently be under the close supervision of the politicians. By contrast many of the most significant steps in French economic policy were taken by the administrative elite without any debate in the French parliament. In many respects the French administrative elite is Burnhamite in character. It is technically very highly qualified, being recruited from the best products of the *Ecole des Sciences politiques* and, since the Second World War, the *Ecole Nationale d'Administration* and, on the technical side, from the *Ecole polytechnique*. Moreover, these are also the sources of top industrial and business management. There is a frequent exchange of personnel between the private and the public sectors. A common career pattern is for some of the most highly qualified civil service recruits to transfer to private management after a decade in public administration.[50]

This administrative elite is quite small in numbers and represents the very cream of the French educational system – the *Polytechnique*, for instance, takes only 200 entrants per annum. All these institutions, and in particular the *Polytechnique*, inspire great loyalty on the part of their graduates. They all pass through a course of education very similar in its content and approach; they share a common educational experience, develop their own jargon, come to possess a common administrative style.[51] Former pupils staff the colleges as well as man the services for which the colleges provide the training, thus ensuring the continuity of the technocratic style. Informal communication both between government and industry is consequently very easy, and the task of securing a consensus for national planning amongst the managers of the national economy, of the state enterprises and of private industry is enormously facilitated.[52]

In Britain, too, the civil service has expanded considerably and officials at many levels are granted considerable discretionary powers within limits laid down by statute. Weber's sharp distinction between political policy-making and the execution of policy does not apply to the higher levels of the British civil service who are expected to assist in the formulation of policy. In this they do more than provide the necessary information for their political masters. Departments offer ministers their own suggestions for new courses of action, and indeed some departments appear to have consistent policies which survive governments of different political persuasions.

These powers certainly make the civil service a 'strategic elite' of great significance in the British power structure. It is not, however, yet in the dominant position which Burnham envisaged and which the French administrative elite attained under the Fourth Republic. Its power is counter-balanced by a stable and effective political authority. Ultimate responsibility still lies with the government, and once political decisions are reached the official becomes the impartial administrator of Weber's model. The doctrine and the fact of political accountability constrains the civil servant by requiring him to mould his advice to the political persuasion – and the political status – of his minister and by the need to provide answers to parliamentary questions ranging from the trivial to the penetrating.

The USA presents the extreme contrast amongst Western democracies to the French situation. Though departmental officials have been very influential on American policy, these should in the main be regarded as members of the political rather than the administrative elite. The very highest officials tend to be political appointees who, even if they were businessmen or academics rather than professional politicians by career, are attached to the political party in power. Career civil servants, though forming a higher proportion of officials than in years past, have a much lower status than in other countries.

The generalisations of Weber and Burnham have been fruitful in providing clues as to the nature of one of the potentially most influential elites in modern politics. The actual power of the bureaucratic elite, however, varies greatly, as we have seen, from the quasi-Burnhamite manager-administrators of France or the European Economic Commission to the politically dominated service of the USA. Power in actual cases can only be ascertained by the study of historical instances. One needs in this, as in all attempts at the attribution of power to groups, to beware of the fallacy of aggregation by which evidence of the planning powers of French officials, the policy-forming opportunities of British civil servants and the independence of the old German officialdom are compounded to produce a picture of the political power of bureaucracy as such.[53]

EDUCATION AND ELITE FORMATION

There is obviously an intimate connection between the educational system of a country and its elite. Educational theories and reforms inevitably have political implications since part of any education is to fit a person out as a member of a body politic whether as a member of a ruling class, a quiescent subject of an administrative state, or a fully participating citizen in some idealised democracy. For the individualist the task of education is to cultivate the independent moral agent, self-reliant and suspicious of accepting the judgment of others in intellectual, moral or political matters. For the traditionalist, by contrast, education inculcates a person into an established discipline which is social as well as intellectual, and the code of which is to be discovered in the achievements of the relevant authorities. The often-heard plea that education should be 'taken out of politics' misunderstands the nature of both activities – education is political through and through. One broad, if in practice over-sharp, distinction between educational systems is between those that aim at producing an elite and those which aim to extend a high level of education to all or to encourage a more cohesive society based on a shared culture. Though in both cases the schools attempt to impart knowledge and skills, these skills are related to the nature of the society desired.

In recent years both elitist and egalitarian forms of education have had their advocates, particularly in Britain where the educational system has been undergoing reappraisal. The process of reappraisal has inevitably led to comparisons being made with the educational systems of other countries. The public sector of education in the USA in particular has afforded a striking contrast to the system adopted by Britain until recent years. Amidst the welter of literature on this topic an older article by Ralph H. Turner[54] still provides one of the best frameworks within which to assess the elitist character of an educational system. Turner outlines two 'ideal types' to which educational systems may approximate and which also operate as norms which people in the system follow, thereby reinforcing the existing system. In the first type – 'contest mobility' – the elite is open to any person who is successful in a contest in which all may enter and in which all are kept in the race for as long as possible. The most able are not segregated from an early age but continue in the same school with the same curriculum as the others. Crucial hurdles are avoided so as to give everyone the maximum opportunity to reach the top of the educational ladder by entering university. It puts a premium on ambition and effort, and the elite is composed of those who are seen to have merited membership by attaining goals understood by all and which all have had the chance to attain. In the alternative type – 'sponsored mobility' – the criteria for elite membership are only fully understood by those who are already members. The aim of the system is not so much the creation of a larger, well-educated elite with a wide range of skills as the filling of limited vacancies in the established elite. The elite 'sponsors' new members by determining the qualifications for membership – ability at classical languages, mastering legal precedents or Chinese calligraphy. The authorities in the art assess the performance of the aspirants. Training for elite positions is highly specialised and involves the selection and segregation of the potential leaders at an early age. Those not believed capable of attaining the qualifications laid down are hived off to schools where opportunities for education in the requisite elite skills are very few, and instead training is given in the less influential and prestigious functions.

The two elites will clearly contrast in nature and size. In Britain, identified by Turner with the pattern of sponsored mobility, there will on this view be either a single elite or a recognised elite hierarchy. The inner core of the educational elite will be small – a point confirmed in the British instance by any measuring rod used, whether the 6 per cent of the population who attend public schools or the 5 per cent who attend university. To enter the elite an aspirant will need to qualify in subjects esteemed by the elite, such as the traditional disciplines of classical languages and literature or history in which the elite members had themselves been educated. The sponsorship mobility model also suggests that entry to the elite is only possible through the elite schools. Evidence is frequently adduced to support claims that such is the case in Britain. The public schools provide almost 60 per cent of company directors, over 70 per cent of Conservative MPs, almost 50 per cent of the 'Great and the Good' who are appointed to Royal Commissions and public inquiries. Graduates of Oxford and Cambridge hold nearly half the posts in the higher civil service and gain 80 per cent of the places filled by competitive entry; provide 30 per cent of MPs.

The 'contest mobility' model, by contrast, suggests that there is no single unified elite or elite hierarchy able to determine entry qualifications. In the USA, Turner's instance of a 'contest mobility' system, a college degree may be desirable for an aspirant to elite status, but this is a qualification which the school system keeps open to a wide section of the population. Neither subject nor place of study are prerequisites for elite membership in a contest system. It is for the aspirant to establish his claims by his own efforts.

As ideal types the two systems are, of course, over-drawn and for this reason do not fit the contrasting systems of Britain and the USA with complete exactness. No-one imagines that even the most elite sectors of the British educational system totally exclude an element of competition nor that all American colleges are open to all-comers. The model also unduly emphasises the importance of education for entry to the elite. Certain strategic elites – such as union leaderships – do not specify educational qualifications for entry, and the best educated of men may be excluded from an elite group on grounds of class, wealth or race. Education has to be seen as one factor amongst others in elite formation and cannot, in particular, be entirely isolated from the class structure. The higher levels of education in both 'contest' and 'sponsored' systems tends to be one of the advantages enjoyed by the wealthier classes.

Both the elite structure and the educational system in Britain are almost certainly less unified than Turner suggests by his identification of Britain with sponsorship mobility. While many commentators have, like Turner, regarded the state grammar schools and the public schools as part of the same elite education, others have discerned a divide between the competitive grammar system and the aristocratic public schools.[55] By comparison with the egalitarianism of the American high school system, the British public schools and state grammar schools must appear distinctly elitist, admitting as they do only 25 per cent of the country's schoolboys. It does not, however, follow that all members of this privileged minority share the same attitudes and the same opportunities to gain positions of wealth and influence. There can be more antagonism between the products of the state and the private sectors of education than between the educationally privileged and the bulk of the population which has pursued a course of education limited both in scope and duration, and has thereby been excluded permanently from many positions of influence.

The egalitarianism of the contest mobility system is, moreover, misleading. Equality of opportunity, it has frequently been said, offers an equal opportunity to become unequal. The extreme case is a 'meritocracy' where the pupil rises on the basis of competitive examination, and where educational qualifications are necessary for every elite position. Intellectuals such as Karl Mannheim have regarded such a society as necessary for the intelligent direction of national planning. Educationists such as Lord James have regarded it as educationally natural to reward intellect and socially desirable in a democracy to cultivate a leadership of talent rather than one of birth. Critics of meritocracy, on the other hand, have alleged that it will encourage intellectual arrogance on the part of the ruling caste.[56] Communication between rulers and ruled will prove impossible where the masses both are and know themselves to be inferior intellectually. The only possible relation will be a manipulative one, with the elite either coercing the majority or moving it by propaganda which appeals to emotion, not reason.[57] Having no common ground with the rest of the society, the meritocrats will be unable to integrate the community, which will in consequence be as divided as under a class structure based on birth or wealth. The usual alternative proposed is an educational system which pays less attention to cultivating an intellectual elite than to providing a general education shared by all, which would form the basis for a greater sense of community. Both educational theories thus remain political and social theories centring on opposed attitudes to elites.

THE 'ESTABLISHMENT'

The 'establishment' is one of the most difficult of specialised elites to detect, describe and assess. Even those who most insist on its presence at the heart of British decision-making and affirm its deleterious effect on national policy-making are unable to identify the establishment with a group which is in any way formally organised. The establishment does not set examination papers for entry; it does not hold annual general meetings or elect a chairman; it does not issue policy-statements or press hand-outs. Since its revival by the journalist, Henry Fairlie, in the 1950s 'establishment' has become a vogue word in Britain. It has been used loosely to refer to the traditional upper classes, the older members of any society or institution that happens to be under discussion, a number of institutions in British life which lie outside democratic control or even the most eminent of a given activity, thereby identifying 'establishment' with 'specialised elite'. These definitions are often unclear and certainly inconsistent with one another. Since no universally accepted definition of the establishment exists the only alternative is to offer a description which by incorporating the highest common factor of the many rival accounts will at least approximate to the amorphous group which so many writers have attempted to identify. It will in a sense be a 'working defini-tion'. It should then be possible to indicate the kinds of evidence which would be required to identify the establishment at work.

In the first place the establishment is not to be identified with one particular specialised elite. Nearly all commentators seem agreed that the national establish-ment incorporates several groups and institutions. It is preferable to speak, as Blondel does,[58] of the establishment as a network of contacts between certain groups of people. Certain groups and bodies would appear from most descriptions to be *ex officio* members – products of the major public schools, the landed aris-tocracy, directors of the leading financial institutions of the City of London, the BBC, the Fellows of the Royal Academy. About others, such as members of the Conservative party, higher civil servants, or *The Times* newspaper, there is rather less certainty as to their membership. Still others, such as self-made businessmen, trades union leaders, prominent engineers, professional sportsmen, are clearly out-side the circle of the establishment. What distinguishes this establishment circle is its access to and use of a network of largely informal contacts. Such contacts stem primarily from family connections – very important in City of London banking – or a shared educational background at public school or at Oxford or Cambridge. This is not to deny, of course, that outsiders may not enter the circle especially through one of the *ex officio* institutions such as the BBC. The contacts are main-tained largely in an informal manner by membership of the London clubs, by the social round of dinners and parties as well as, more formally, in business meetings and at official events.

Membership of the establishment could, in principle, be determined by the access a person or group has to such contacts. This could clearly vary from peri-od to period. *The Times* newspaper features prominently in accounts of this world as it was immediately before the Second World War, but it is possible that in recent years it has not been so close to this particular elite circle. Not all members of a predominantly establishment group are necessarily members of the establishment. By their social and educational background most Conservative MPs would have ready access to the network but this would not necessarily be true of one who was grammar-school-educated, middle class, with business or professional training, even if he were in the inner leadership of the party. Similarly, whilst many higher civil servants, particularly at the Foreign Office, have the social and educational background of the typical 'establishment' figure, the majority do not, and their more formal methods of business and style of life will be less likely to take them into the establishment channels of communication. The network may also be limited territorially. To some commentators the 'establishment' is English rather than British, and others believe its operations to be confined to London and its region,[59] which would exclude some of the landed aristocracy from membership.

The principal use made of this network of contacts is to mobilise opinion on certain kinds of public issue and to recruit new members for associated elites such as the City, the army and, especially in the past, the Church of England.[60] Evidence for such a world of informal contacts and pressures tends only to become available well after the meetings and conversations have taken place when they are recorded in the diaries and memoirs of the eminent. The autobiographies and papers of the participants in the events surrounding the abdication of King Edward VIII provide an excellent example of the informal mechanisms for the expression and formulation of establishment opinion – a round of meetings and social engagements which brought together prime minister, the editor of *The Times*, Archbishop of Canterbury, king's advisers, ambassadors and Commonwealth leaders whose interconnections were based less on the 'institutional proximity' detected in the USA by Wright Mills than on long-standing acquaintanceships.[61] The recently published diaries of Sir Harold Nicolson afford a similar glimpse into the world of the club and into the social connections between political influentials, governors of the BBC and the world of literature.[62] The novels of Evelyn Waugh and in particular of Anthony Powell delineate the same world with only the bare minimum of farce or irony necessary to translate fact into fiction.

If any account of the nature of the establishment must be impressionistic, exact measurement of its influence on British politics is still more difficult. Many of its members are men of influence but their influence stems not from their contacts with the establishment but from their positions in associated elites. Establishment status is not the key to the power of a conservative minister or the influence of the Governor of the Bank of England. The likely success of the establishment in its use of the network to influence political decisions may also depend on which party holds office. On the account given above of the establishment, its members permeate – but do not monopolise – the Conservative party but are little represented in the Labour party. A Conservative government may ignore the views sent along the establishment's communications network, but the network may not even reach a Labour government. It is also extremely difficult to predict the sorts of issues which will now lead to the mobilisation of establishment opinion other than to say that they are more likely to be 'social' issues than 'political' or 'economic'. Establishment membership, as it has been defined here, is not representative of all shades of opinion on economic or political matters. At the same time its network includes more than the political or financial elites which come partly within it.

It may be that the establishment can only lay claim to being a social elite as the defender of values which are, or once were, thought worthy of imitation by other sections of the community. Certain innovations are seen as threatening moral and social values of which the establishment claims to act as guardian. The introduction of commercial television appears to have been one such innovation which stimulated opposition from most of the quarters identified with the establishment.[63] Such concerted interventions do, however, presuppose a degree of unity amongst the establishment which may no longer exist (if it ever did) as fewer social issues arouse the moral certainty felt in earlier generations. The introduction of commercial television also illustrates the fact that the establishment cannot be taken to be either a 'ruling class' with the economic power to forestall changes to which it is opposed or a 'power elite' with a veto-power over legislation. Commercial television was introduced by a Conservative government despite establishment opposition. Despite the 'conspiracy theories' that see the establishment as the covert ruling elite of the country it is difficult to interpret the establishment as anything other than a broad 'strategic elite' which the political elite and other elites must take into account when formulating policies, canvassing support and making decisions.

ELITE CONSENSUS

It is a possibility that the informal social connections characteristic of an establishment are giving way in Britain to an approximation to the system of 'institutional proximity' that Mills detected in the USA. The establishment may reflect a more unified age when a single class with shared background could man the leading positions of state and when industry was less directly concerned in government. Now under, say, a Labour government, decisions on the central issues concerning politics and the economy are likely to be taken by non-establishment figures from Labour party, Civil Service, trade union movement and industry. The City's influence is not the result of its establishment position. Their institutional proximity by no means necessarily gives rise to a united policy on the part of all participants. At the same time Britain is a comparatively small country and the leaders of these strategic elites can quickly form acquaintanceships and meet together, not only across the bargaining table but at events ranging from state banquets to academic seminars. It is possible that, while not agreeing on policies, they may share similar views as to the appropriate decision-making process, namely negotiation between elites. The several elites are on this view interconnected by the bargaining process rather than by the social network of the old establishment. One recent commentator, however, has seen the British 'power structure' very differently. Anthony Sampson concluded that the rulers were not at all closely-knit:

> They are not so much in the centre of a solar system, as in a cluster of interlocking circles, each one largely preoccupied with its own professionalism and expertise, and touching others only at one edge...they are not a single Establishment but a ring of Establishments, with slender connections. The frictions and balances between the different circles are the supreme safeguard of democracy. No one man can stand in the centre, for there is no centre.[64]

Sampson detected not a tendency for these circles to coalesce but for them to fly apart.

Sampson's argument is illustrative of one view taken of the relationship between elites by those who believe that modern societies are headed by a plurality of elites. 'Elite competition' and elite specialisation ensure that no inner circle can dominate such a differentiated society. The variety of elites means that more minorities are able to influence events, thereby widening the circle of participation. Competition means that the elected politicians can perform the role of umpire among the claims of the elites, reconciling and modifying these claims in the public interest. Democracy is safeguarded by the range, variety and openness of elites and by the indirect influence accorded to the electorate by the competition between the leadership minorities.

The alternative thesis holds that whilst each specialised elite concerns itself primarily with defending its own interests against other elites there grows up at the same time an attitude towards the process of decision-making – particularly at the national level – which is shared by the otherwise rival elites. The elites come to be committed to a process of decision-making in which only they participate. Industrialists and unionists may meet on opposite sides of a negotiating table. But, within broad limits, they agree on the desirability of the negotiating machinery which limits the circle of bargainers to the 'professionals'. In developed capitalist economies industrialists and unionists also find themselves working side by side on a host of governmental advisory and planning committees which bring them into the closest contact with the political elite, top civil servants, the leaders of finance and so on. They sit on these committees less as representatives of antagonistic interests than as experts working as colleagues for the national interest. They may as a result become imbued with an ethic of 'responsibility' which brings them closer to one another but which may open a gap between each elite and the sectional interest of which it is the leader. Industrialists and unionists are then to be found joined with politicians in exhorting industry and labour to respect agreements negotiated by the national leaderships and even to accept sacrifices for the sake of the 'public interest'. In such ways an 'elite consensus' arises on matters of procedure and even on some matters of substance. Hence the accusations frequently made against union leaderships, but not unknown amongst leading industrialists, that the elite has become alienated from its following – that it has become a part of a new 'establishment'.

This style of consensus politics is often alleged to be characteristic of Britain.[65] It differs from the much-discussed consensus politics in America in the mid-1960s. American internal policy aimed at securing the support of the widest range of groups and interests and at meeting the wishes of the broadest public, whether measured by pollsters or the intuition of the politician. 'Elite consensus' aims at involving in policy-formulation and execution only the leaderships of the most important national interest groups. In Britain such involvement occurs very largely in the stage of policy-making prior to the announcement of any governmental action during which 'interests' – i.e. their leaderships – are consulted by civil servants and ministers. Typically this takes place in private, and goes largely unreported by the mass media. Hundreds of committees, some permanent, others *ad hoc*, draw the various elites into the processes of government. Not only the same interest group but the same person will be found sitting on several such bodies.[66]

There is a great tradition of voluntary service in British government which has continued into these days of professional administration. Lay advisers are regularly called in to provide expert counsel or merely to 'represent' the public. There is, however, a tendency for the same laymen to be appointed time and again to a wide variety of committees. No conspiratorial innermost elite need be inferred. Often the 'interests' nominate the same person in order the easier to coordinate their policy recommendations. Civil servants and ministers tend to reappoint men who have already proved cooperative and efficient committeemen. Finally, the fund of such men is not large. The work makes considerable demands on the person's time, and can only be undertaken by the successful self-employed professional man, the businessman who can afford to leave his fellow-directors in charge of his business, or the person whose employers are willing to allow him leave for public service.

Such lay public persons do not, of course, constitute an elite group with a distinct agreed policy of their own on all the issues upon which they advise. Nor is their advice by any means always congenial to the ministers and civil servants who appoint them. But the regularity with which they are involved in the governmental process may compromise their status as 'independents'. They become, in the phrase of one of their number, 'inside outsiders' – in tune with the Whitehall approach to issues even if not in perfect accord with the decisions reached. Involvement and the need for 'responsibility' may mute criticism which ought to be made by the 'representative' of lay opinion. In the extreme case the consultations may involve government secrets which the pressure group leadership cannot divulge to its followers, or the layman to the public at large.[67]

One consequence may be that the consultative process which aims at preparing sensible government action as well as at sounding out opinion will only include those with orthodox opinions. What is interpreted as 'vertical' communication of opinion from ruled to rulers may in fact be 'horizontal' communication from one elite to another. Talk in Britain about the gulf between 'us' and 'them' may reflect this appearance of elite consensus rather than the existence of any unified ruling elite.

As so often in elite theories there can be strong and weak versions of the theory of elite consensus. In its strongest version it approaches a strict ruling elite theory. Elite proximity might be institutionalised as in the corporate state of Fascist theory where the elites of industry, labour, agriculture and so on become virtual governmental agencies. A somewhat weaker situation is that of the inner core of the American 'power elite' as seen by C. Wright Mills. Institutional proximity results in the frequent interchange of roles amongst the topmost leaders. Mills pointed to the regularity and ease with which in the USA business leaders moved into and out of government office from the cabinet downwards.[68]

Parallels can be found in governmental systems as different as those of Britain and France. Even in Britain, where elite specialisation has been strong, there have in recent years been signs of a greater mobility amongst those on the top rungs of the hierarchies. A number of civil servants have resigned to take directorships or chairmanships of industrial companies; very few business leaders have been tempted to accept posts in the administration of national economic planning; prominent politicians have taken positions on the boards of public enterprises and on regional planning bodies, and the occasional union leader has been brought into the government. The significance of such interchanging of roles depends, of course, on the degree of the role differentiation and specialisation in society referred to earlier. There is some dispute as to the accuracy of Wright Mills' thesis that in the USA moves from one elite sphere to another are becoming easier and more frequent. Suzanne Keller and others have asserted that elite members are nowadays more specialised to their particular fields, and reach the top only by spending a life-long career in the one activity.[69] In less differentiated societies the pattern is necessarily different. Developing countries have a smaller pool of highly trained personnel. Activities which have developed as specialisms in Europe and the USA may be more closely integrated in the developing territories, particularly of Africa and Asia. Public enterprise and widespread government intervention in the economy bridge the gap between state and economy and their respective elites which has grown up in Western countries. The importance of the 'managerial elite' may thus be greater in 'developing' than in 'developed' societies. The manager-administrators seldom constitute a ruling elite, however, even in the developing nations. Ultimate authority lies with either the political elite composed of the nationalist parties which took over from the colonial administration or, increasingly, with a 'military' government.

This thesis of role-interchangeability then shades off into the still weaker theory that consensus arises from elite cooperation which in turn may be a consensus about the substance of policy or merely about procedures. Competing elites, finally, may agree at least on the rules according to which they compete, whether the rules of the market or the rules of democratic choice. The difference between a situation of elite competition and that of elite consensus or even elite domination can appear to be a difference of degree. Sometimes the differences turn out to be terminological or to arise from the methods of the analyst. But often differences of degree are differences of real substance.

NOTES

1   See below, pp. 88–9.

2   For a range of such theories in both place and time see C. Hill, 'The Norman Yoke' in *Puritanism and Revolution*, Secker and Warburg, London, 1958; M. Anderson, 'The Myth of the 'Two Hundred Families'', *Political Studies*, XIII, 2, June, 1965, pp. 163–78; R.

Hofstadter, *The Paranoid Style in American Politics*, Knopf, New York, 1966.

3 It is constructed from a number of sources. Suzanne Keller, *Beyond the Ruling Class*, Random House, New York, 1963, is a good example.

4 Yale University Press, New Haven, 1961.

5 *Elites in Latin America*, (eds S. M. Lipset and A. Solari), Oxford University Press, New York, 1967, pp. 117–45.

6 Scott's description suggests that the Marxist term 'ruling class' would be more appropriate.

7 Allen Potter, *Organized Groups in British National Politics*, Faber, London, 1961.

8 Potter, Ch. 5.

9 Potter, Ch. 7.

10 *Who Governs?* pp. 181–3 and *passim*.

11 *Who Governs?* pp. 184–9.

12 See above, pp. 40–1.

13 See Ch. 5 for a discussion of the many complicating factors.

14 See *From Max Weber* (eds H. H. Gerth and C. Wright Mills), Routledge, London, 1948, pp. 186–94.

15 *From Max Weber*, p. 193.

16 For a contrary view, see S. Keller, *Beyond the Ruling Class*, Random House, New York, 1963, p. 20.

17 See W. G. Runciman, *Relative Deprivation and Social Justice*, Routledge, London, 1966, Ch. III, on this and for a clear treatment of class, status and power.

18 See Nelson W. Polsby, *Community Power and Political Theory*, University Press, Yale, New Haven, 1963, pp. 100–4 and the further discussion below in Ch.5.

19 From Max Weber, pp. 190 ff.

20 'The Concept of Social Elites', *International Social Science Bulletin*, Vol. 8, 1956, pp. 413–24.

21 J. Blondel, *Voters, Parties and Leaders*, Penguin, Harmondsworth, 1963, p. 254. See also W. L. Guttsman, *The British Political Elite*, Macgibbon and Kee, London, 1963, p. 370.

22 See R. A. Dahl and C. E. Lindblom, *Politics, Economics and Welfare*, Harper, New York, 1953.

23 *Elites in Latin America* (eds Lipset and Solari), p. 120.

24 S. Aaronovitch, *The Ruling Class*, Lawrence and Wishart, London, 1961, p. 149.

25 R. Aron, 'Social Structure and the Ruling Class', *British Journal of Sociology*, Vol. 1, No. 1–2 (1950) pp. 1–16 and 126–43.

26 Dahl, *Modern Political Analysis*, Prentice-Hall, Englewood Cliffs, 1963, pp. 35–38.

27 Keller, *Beyond the Ruling Class*, p. 20 and *passim*.

28 *Higher Civil Servants in Britain*, Routledge, London, 1955.

29 *The New Men of Power*, Harcourt Brace, New York, 1948.

30 *The Soviet Bureaucratic Elite*, Stevens, London, 1959.

31 Galaxy edition, Oxford University Press, New York, 1964.

32 See below, pp. 107-8.

33 *The Man on Horseback*, Pall Mall Press, London, 1962.

34 Free Press, New York, 1960.

35 Macmillan, New York, 1932.

36 Sweet and Maxwell, London, 1961.

37 See Florence, *Ownership, Control, etc.*, pp. 92–100.

38 *Ownership, Control, etc.*, p. 192.

39 Florence, *Ownership, Control, etc.*, pp. 88–9.

40 See Barratt-Brown, 'The Controllers', *Universities and Left Review*, Autumn 1958, pp. 53–61.

41 E.g., the then chairman of I.C.I., Sir Alexander Fleck, a chemist turned manager, is cited by Barratt-Brown as a banking-nominee on I.C.I. because of his seat on the board of a bank

42 See P. Ferris, *The City*, Penguin, Harmondsworth, 1962, Ch. 5.

43 *The Eighteenth Brumaire of Louis Bonaparte*, Marx and Engels, *Selected Works*, Vol. 1, Lawrence and Wishart, London, 1958.

44 Some of the details are to be found in S. Brittan, *The Treasury under the Tories*, 1951–1964, Penguin, Harmondsworth, 1964, pp. 215–22.

45 *The Power Elite*, Chs. 6–7.

46 On Britain see G. H. Copeman, *Leaders of British Industry*, Gee, London, 1955; R. V. Clements, *Managers*, Allen & Unwin, London, 1958; Acton Society Trust, *Management Succession*, London, 1958; D. Clark, *The Industrial Manager*, Business Publications, London, 1966. On the USA, see Mills, *The Power Elite*; Keller, *Beyond the Ruling Class*, pp. 307–24; W. L. Warner and J. C. Abegglen, *Big Business Leaders in America*, Harper, New York, 1955.

47 Florence, *Ownership, Control, etc.*, p. 187.

48 See above, pp. 15–7.

49 Weber, 'Politics as a Vocation', *From Max Weber*, (eds Gerth and Mills), Routledge, London, 1948, p. 95.

50 See D. Granick, *The European Executive*, Doubleday, Garden City, N.Y., 1962, Ch. 5.

51 See H. Parris, 'Twenty Years of l'Ecole Nationale d'Administration', *Public Administration*, 43, 1965, pp. 407–9.

52 For an excellent brief review of French technocrats in government see F. F. Ridley, 'French Technocracy and Comparative Government', *Political Studies*, XIV, No.1, Feb. 1966, pp. 34–52.

53 See below, p. 107.

54 'Sponsored and Contest Mobility and the School System', *American Sociological Review*, Dec. 1960, pp. 855–67.

55 See A. Sampson, *Anatomy of Britain*, Hodder and Stoughton, London, 1962. Also the contrasting interpretations of Halsey, Brown and Holbrook in articles in *New Left Review*, Sept.–Oct. 1916.

56 Michael Young's satire, *The Rise of the Meritocracy*, Thames and Hudson, London, 1958, amusingly elaborates this point.

57 Cp. Hannah Arendt, 'What is Authority?', *Between Past and Future*, Faber, London, 1961, on this problem in Plato, pp. 91–141.

58 Voters, Parties and Leaders, Penguin, 1963, Ch. 9.

59 See W. J. M. Mackenzie on the 'leadership sub-system' based on the 'South Eastern 'heartland'', *Politics and Social Science*, Penguin, Harmondsworth, 1967, pp. 351–2.

60 And, it appears, to recruit spies. See B. Page, D. Leitch & P. Knightly, *Philby: The Spy who Betrayed a Generation*, Deutsch, London, 1968.

61 See, e.g., G. Wrench, *Geoffrey Dawson and our Times*, Hutchinson, London, 1955, Ch. XXIX. *History of The Times*, Vol. IV, Pt. II, pp. 1027–1048. Thomas Jones, *A Diary with*

Letters, 1931–1950, Oxford University Press, London, 1964, pp. 279–97.

62 H. Nicolson, *Harold Nicolson: Diaries and Letters, 1939–1945*. Collins, London, 1967. See also *Chips: The Diaries of Sir Henry Channon*, Weidenfeld and Nicolson, London, 1967.

63 See H. H. Wilson, *Pressure Group*, Secker and Warburg, London, 1961.

64 *Anatomy of Britain*, Hodder and Stoughton, London, 1962, p. 624.

65 See J. P. Nettl, 'Consensus or Elite Domination: The Case of Business', *Political Studies*, XIII, 1, Feb. 1965, pp. 22–44.

66 See Political and Economic Planning, *Advisory Committees in British Government*, 1960, and 'Government by Appointment', *Planning*, XXVI (1960), No. 443.

67 See Potter, *Organized Groups in British National Politics*, p. 99, and Ch.12, on the working of the consultative process.

68 See also Allen Potter, 'The American Governing Class', *British Journal of Sociology*, XIII, 4, Dec. 1962, pp. 309–19.

69 Keller, *Beyond the Ruling Class*, pp. 212–13.

chapter four | empirical tests of elitist theories

One of the essential tasks of any elitist is to establish the degree to which any given elite is cohesive, conscious and 'conspiratorial'. Similarly it is incumbent upon any elite pluralist to assess the nature and extent of either competition or consensus amongst leadership groups where a number of elites have been identified. The major elite theories were often weak on these points. There was a tendency to assert rather than prove that the dominant group or groups in a society were bound together by ties of common interest, shared values or similar upbringing. This fault may be found both in the 'classical elitists' and in their Marxist opponents. Mosca suggests that the middle class character of his 'political class' will make for a certain unity amongst its members but, for the most part, he merely asserts that the fact of minority itself will ensure the elite's unity and singleness of purpose.

James Burnham asserted that industrial managers and public administrators would be in basic agreement on the fundamentals of policy in a 'managerial society' by virtue of the technocratic nature of the work which would be common to both. Burnham pays little attention to the possibility of clashes of interest between managers in the coal industry and those in the oil industry, or between industrial managers and state bureaucrats. He pays still less heed to the possibility of conflicts of principle within the managerial class itself since on his view the shared experience of its members will determine their shared attitudes.

The Marxist is not required by his theory to establish the conspiratorial character of the ruling class. Indeed, the ruling class is not in ultimate control of its own destiny. The downfall of the capitalist class is in large part the unintended outcome of many thousands of isolated actions by individual capitalists competing against one another. Nevertheless the Marxist also holds that a ruling class is cohesive and conscious of itself as a class. It both has objective interests and a subjective awareness of its position, its opportunities and of the threats to which it is exposed from classes whose interests are objectively opposed to its own. It may on occasions consciously and deliberately take steps to confirm its economic supremacy through the exercise of state power and by its use of ideology. More often Marx suggests that class consciousness and cohesion arise in a more subtle manner through the conditioning force of the economic process. Either way one is allowed to infer the existence and the cohesiveness of the ruling class from the economic relationships in the society.

'Social being determines consciousness' in the sense of determining a society's horizons of experience. In capitalist societies individualism, natural rights and liberty under law are defended as universal moral and political principles. They are at the same time ideals which facilitate economic production and exchange, and help bolster the dominance of the ruling class although this fact is not necessarily one of which the ideologists are directly conscious. The capitalist economy is essentially individualist and, the argument continues, this ensures that political thought under capitalism cannot but reflect on and elaborate the political implications of individualism. This is typical of the way in which political and social attitudes are shaped by the economic process. In the Marxist view a person's class position is, in the bulk of cases, a precise indicator of his general attitudes although not necessarily of his precise detailed policies.

The *a priori* character of such assertions has, understandably, led to criticism. The conclusions drawn about the political attitudes of elite groups and classes is clearly presupposed in the assumptions. Is it, however, a necessary truth that no class or elite can act in a disinterested or even altruistic fashion? Alternatively, if it is insisted that the vast majority of political conduct is self-interested, it may yet be the case that an elite's rational perception of its own interest may lead it into following a course of action in line with many of the interests of its opponents. Such flexibility is, on the whole, deemed impossible by Marxists, the ruling class being as much the victim as the manipulator of social tendencies. It would, however, be one of the marks of a successful elite, in Mosca's view. This adaptability nevertheless makes more difficult the task of predicting inevitable clashes of opinion between elite and non-elite, or among elite groups on the basis of their respective positions in society.

Recent years have seen a great amount of empirical research on elites aiming to portray the nature of either particular specialised elites or the degree of integration displayed by a national elite. Such research seeks to replace the assertions of elite theorists by some 'hard' data to test, where possible, 'hypotheses' suggested by the grand theories.

The methodologies adopted in these investigations can, with few exceptions, be brought under four broad headings:
  (i) the study of institutional positions, about which much has already been said in discussing the work of C. Wright Mills;
 (ii) the examination of the social background and recruitment patterns of elites;
(iii) the 'reputational' approach associated chiefly with Floyd Hunter; and
 (iv) the study of the 'decision-making process' associated chiefly with Robert A. Dahl. Both the 'reputational' and the 'decision-making' studies have been mainly used in the study of smaller communities – cities and towns – rather than of countries. In very recent years there have been some attempts at synthesising the two approaches.

ELITE BACKGROUND AND RECRUITMENT

It is a widespread assumption of political sociology that the social background and upbringing of a decision-maker will influence his attitudes and policies. To a limited extent this assumption is, it seems, shared by electors who sometimes argue that, say, a candidate's working class background will ensure that he will be sympathetic to the claims of the working class, and that a rival upper-class candidate will be correspondingly ignorant of the problems and unmoved by the wishes of the workers. Hence there is a tendency, more marked in some countries than others, for parties to nominate candidates who, in their own social background, are 'representative' of the predominant background of the local electorate.

Behind such assumptions and practices is the belief that no political participant ever approaches a decision without bias. This bias may not be sinister or even conscious. The future member of an elite may receive his first induction into politics in early childhood from his parents, his teachers or friends. These experiences may even make him a lifelong adherent of one party, and there is a considerable body of evidence revealing the frequency with which 'like father, like son' aptly describes voting behaviour. Party allegiance may, however, be less important than a more generalised attitude to politics and to social opportunities imbibed in early life. A person may come to feel that persons of his sort of family background or with his level of education are underprivileged relative to others. This impression of injustice may inspire him to seek to rectify it by entering politics himself. Alternatively, and here the limits of background analysis reveal themselves, he may be resigned to political impotence and live out his days in the 'mass' or 'non-elite'.

While our future leaders may learn attitudes to authority, liberty, participation and so on in childhood, this is not to say that such attitudes can never be changed. The process of 'political socialisation' is a continuing one and the rising politician or businessman or unionist may well alter his outlook fundamentally during his career. One of the major claims made by those who have advocated the extension of the franchise and the widening of political opportunities has been that participation will provide an education in political responsibility. Facing a practical political decision, like 'meeting a payroll' in industry, as well as giving the participant a sense of personal involvement is often seen as a cure for the proponent of the 'easy solution' – particularly, perhaps, when it is of a radical nature. It has already been remarked that participation in national decisions by erstwhile rival elites may draw the elites closer together and bind them in a new 'ethic of responsibility'.

The factors in a person's lifetime which can affect his political and social attitudes are very numerous. He may imbibe long-standing traditional attitudes. His whole political conduct may reflect the impact of some notable event which affected most men of his generation. The attitudes of many of the political leaders of Britain in the twenty years since the Second World War were profoundly influenced by their pre-war experience of the depression years, or by their reaction to the policy of appeasement. In some cases a forceful personality, a teacher, an established senior politician or a successful industrial magnate can shape the outlook of an aspirant to elite position by offering him a model of wisdom, skill and enterprise – *virtù*, as Machiavelli termed it. A person may carry such predispositions with him for a long time, sometimes for long after the circumstances which gave rise to them have ceased to be relevant to the issues before him. These predispositions serve as frameworks within which the political or economic world is viewed. Often they limit what is seen so that it fits in with the person's preconceptions, each new experience going only to confirm what was already believed.

The extent to which this happens may also depend upon the 'civic culture' of a society. In some countries, bound by tradition or with comparatively little social mobility, most of the factors influencing attitudes to society and politics will point in the same direction and reinforce what the person learned in his early years. In such societies individuals tend to follow the same paths as their fathers, or at least hold the same status in the society. In other societies where mobility is much greater or where there exists a multiplicity of cultures rivalling one another for the attention of the individual there is a greater likelihood of his altering his attitudes quite radically during his lifetime as well as of his differing quite markedly from the views of earlier generations of his family.

Many influences are highly individual and unpredictable and even where a generation experiences a major event such as the fall of France, its leaders and potential leaders react in quite contrasting ways, whether by – in this particular case – collaborating with the victors, joining the Vichy regime, or opting for de Gaulle or for Communism. Nevertheless, students of political behaviour have believed that certain factors, particularly class and education, are especially significant in shaping attitudes and policies. These factors have consequently been widely studied as indices of the potential allegiance of individuals to political parties and interest groups. It is not anticipated that every individual of a given class or schooling will develop identical attitudes in adult life, but it is anticipated that significant correlations between background and political behaviour will emerge. Moreover it is a widely held view that a shared social and educational background substantially promotes the cohesiveness of any elite group.

The City of London is a classic instance. The financial institutions of the City of London are staffed heavily by products of the public school system – the 'public school proletariat', as Anthony Sampson terms them.[1] Posts are filled on the 'old boy network' and whom you know is all-important. This state of affairs is far from being thought deplorable by City men. It is instead justified as essential to the City's way of business. Verbal promises, in personal meeting or by telephone, constitute the basis of a large part of City transactions. Money is made and lost by assessing the confidence of the other party, which is displayed in a turn of phrase or an air of determination or indecision in making a bargain. Acceptance of the motto 'my word is my bond' speeds business and permits the City to dispense with the legal apparatus of other financial centres. For the utterance of a promise to be taken as an obligation to perform the bargain there must be a considerable degree of trust, and this, City men declare, most readily arises where all parties speak a common 'language' – in words, accent, gestures, dress – which the parties know before they begin dealings rather than acquire in the job. On the basis of this agreed etiquette, the parties watch for signs of the drift of business – a facial expression, a phrase, a public school joke which may inadvertently reveal the person's bargaining position, or be a kite flown to find the point of settlement.[2]

To call such a language 'jargon' would give too technical an impression of talk which apparently may be as much about cricket as about money, but the function it serves is much the same as that served by jargon – it facilitates the form of business and possesses a mystique which in this case is attached to a class and an education as well as to a job. Many public schools have their own 'private languages' – Winchester's with its 'bad Notions' like 'sporting a loather' has been described recently by T. Bishop and R. Wilkinson[3] – and the City's, though much less esoteric, is an extension of the same cult.

The City of London is often described as a village in which everyone of any importance knows everyone else of any importance. Personal contact is essential to the City's mode of doing business and it is furthered not only by common class and school background but also by overlapping membership on the boards of directors and by the frequency of family businesses and family connections between different firms. In view of the nature of City business, involving assessing confidence, rendering financial advice and raising funds, the existence of overlapping board membership – merchant bankers sitting on the boards of other banks, insurance companies and industrial firms – is perfectly understandable and sensible. It reflects no sinister conspiracy. If banks are to service industry they need these contacts.

More relevant to the immediate issue is the striking survival of the family business into modern economic conditions where, according to a Weber or a Burnham, they should be inappropriate. Some such City businesses have become public companies for legal and tax purposes, but they have retained financial and executive control in the hands of the family. Hambro's is directed by the Hambro family, members of the Rothschild family are directors of Rothschild's and Schroder's and Baring's are similarly directed by members of the family, although officially they are public companies. Some families, such as the Barings and the Smiths, appear on numerous city and industrial boards, holding the chairmanships in several.[4]

In September 1957 these interconnections of City firms became a matter of public comment when widespread rumours circulated which suggested that highly profitable sales of gilt-edged were made a day or so before Bank Rate rose and that these sales were made because the news of the projected increase had been leaked. Suspicion fell on firms and individuals holding overlapping directorships in the Bank of England and in banking houses which had completed successful sales of stock in the days preceding the rise in Bank Rate. The upshot was a tribunal of enquiry which shed light on the informal methods of working in the City – the 'parlour' in which partners work and deliberate until a policy emerges, the personal contacts with other bankers and with politicians, the attempts at estimating the mood of such contacts. There was the grouse shooting holiday during which business was not discussed, but nevertheless the mood of a junior minister in the party was duly noted in letters on the financial crisis.

The tribunal stimulated academic reactions. Lupton and Wilson undertook research into the origins and connections between financial, administrative and political circles.[5] They constructed twenty-three 'family trees', each connecting with other trees and revealing family links between the directors of the leading city businesses, industrialists and the Conservative Party leadership. The vast majority of City directors had received a public school education with six leading schools providing 66 per cent of Bank of England directors and 43 per cent of the directors of City firms. It was an educational background which again gave them much in common with the members of the Conservative government.

Nevertheless the tribunal concluded that despite such opportunities for conspiracy no word or action had been untoward. The participants had scrupulously maintained the distinction between their roles as public advisers and private businessmen.[6] In one instance a banker's partners refrained from involving him in deliberations which might embarrass him or force him to give a hint of what he knew as a Bank of England director. Search into the background and values of this elite could only reveal its potentialities for common, conspiratorial action. It would not indicate that conspiracy would inevitably occur. Individuals do not necessarily owe a primary allegiance to others of their own social status or who hold their own beliefs. They may place public responsibility above their private interests. Alternatively, the values acquired by family tradition or 'on the job' by a prominent City leader may include a sense of responsibility to the wider community which is respected by others in his immediate circle. In such cases 'background' points in more than one direction. Even family connections need not be decisive in making for policy agreement. Family quarrels are not unknown, and the allegiance to family does not necessarily withstand allegiance to a principle.

There are, therefore, many limitations to the enterprise of inferring elite attitudes and policies from social and educational background, but this is not to say that the study of background offers no advantages. It can illuminate the very different styles of recruitment to elite position which can occur within a single society. In France educational achievement is the key to high position in governmental administration, and to most top managerial positions in industry and business. In Britain recruitment to the civil service on the basis of open competitive examination contrasts strongly with the family and school sponsorship so characteristic of the City of London.[7]

The study of elite background on the whole tells more about the society in which the elite exists than the policies or politics which the elite will pursue. That the upper and upper middle classes and the products of a small number of educational institutions provide such a substantial proportion of the elites of Britain, France and America is certainly indicative of the opportunities in these countries. It does not necessarily suggest that the various elites will be in agreement with one

another – still less that the elites of these different countries will share similar values, since nationality can be a more important factor than social background in
influencing attitudes.[8]

How far the elite is a microcosm of society in its social composition is frequently discussed in studies of elite background. Jean Blondel has made this a
central theme of his *Voters, Parties and Leaders*. He inquires into the extent to
which political parties, interest groups and civil servants in Britain are 'representative' of the social composition of the country at large. This is not a discussion of
the legal conditions for a Member of Parliament to be 'the representative' of his
constituents. The interest in social composition of elite groups stems from the
widely held assumption, as Blondel understands it, that such groups should
approximate in social background, experience – and, hence, views – to those
whom they serve.[9]

Starting with an account of the social structure – proportions of the population
in each social class and status group, each educational category, income group and
employment – it is possible to compare the background of elite members and their
families along several dimensions with the population at large. In nearly all cases
it is found that leaders are not 'representative' of the society. In Parliament the
middle class is over-represented and the public schools contribute a very disproportionate number. Most such inquiries conclude that the activists in any group
tend to possess a higher social status than the mass of the population. Dahl found
this to be true of the sub-leadership stratum in New Haven, as did Agger, Goldrich
and Swanson in their studies of four different American communities. Voting studies in America and elsewhere have established that the higher a person's social status and economic class, and the longer his education, the more likely he is to be a
political activist whether at the minimal level of voting or at the level of political
office.

Such inequalities of background and in participation do not, of themselves,
turn the activists into a single elite distinct from the rest of the population. They
may still be active in different parties or interest groups, and it is not difficult to
think of activists who have been totally without influence. Nor does the 'unrepresentative' character of elites always cause tension between them and the rest of the
society. An upper class background does not preclude a politician from understanding the demands of less advantaged constituents. Moreover, the 'representative' quality of an elite may not be important to its supporters. Electors may
believe that a politician with a good education and with professional experience –
a lawyer for example – will make more headway in pressing for their interests
than a politician more like themselves in ability. More fundamentally, the electors
may show little concern for the qualities of the candidate and vote entirely according to the party label. Trade unions are certainly concerned that their leaders
should be 'representative' of the social, occupational and educational experience
of their members. By contrast an association of businessmen may prefer to be led
by the delegate from the largest firm in their line of business, believing that a government will be more likely to take into account the views of an industrial giant

than those of a number of small units and also, perhaps, that the big firm can employ the best negotiators.

In some societies the 'representative' character of an elite is complicated by the racial, tribal or ethnic composition of the population. Such societies can often be divided vertically as well as horizontally, and a number of complex social structures are theoretically possible. A frequent cause of tension occurs where one group holds political power whilst business and industry is largely in the hands of another group, often a minority under pressure as a result of its economic role. Each race, tribe or ethnic grouping could have a high degree of autonomy and each be stratified horizontally on social and economic grounds. This relation between the groups, certainly rare in practice, could be designated by the slogan 'separate but equal'. Alternatively one group may hold the dominant position in the political structure. It may yet claim, as the South African government does on occasions, to be according a separate and largely autonomous position for the other groups (although strictly autonomy is impossible where it is ultimately dependent on the will of another). More frequently a state, for instance a former colony recently come to independence, will claim to guarantee equality of opportunity for all. Constitutional guarantees for minorities are considered unnecessary, being infringements of the basic principle of equality. The outcome, however, is very often that elite positions become the monopoly of one race or tribe. Integration frequently proves unsuccessful. The dominant group will, admittedly, usually be the majority grouping and, hence, its dominance is readily justifiable on the principles of majoritarian democracy. At the same time the elite[10] will be 'unrepresentative' of the society. Substantial minorities permanently excluded from the centres of influence can, of course, be the cause of very real tension frequently met by repression on the part of the elite.

Other societies give the appearance of a more pluralistic ethnic – but not necessarily racial – mixture. An example might be the USA where an education in American citizenship has been consciously provided to ensure a more homogeneous population. Despite this, innumerable studies of American history and politics have demonstrated the importance of ethnic politics – of the extent to which an ethnic vote can be 'delivered', of the significance of constructing a coalition of ethnic minorities. Studies of the social backgrounds of leadership groups can trace the emergence of the several ethnic minorities into positions of influence, particularly in politics, and reveal the extent to which the various waves of minorities have been each in its turn 'under-represented' in the elites. Repeated studies have concluded that, despite the efforts at integration, in politics, business, the diplomatic service and amongst the military the elite in America is predominantly, though not exclusively, white, Anglo-Saxon or north-west European by extraction, and protestant.

Perhaps the most thorough-going investigation of a national elite which centres on the study of social background has been John Porter's monumental work on the Canadian elite.[11] Here, too, according to Porter, ethnicity assumes almost as great an importance as the class factor. Canadians of English origin have retained a 'charter status' and are dominant in most elites. Other immigrant groups, including the large French Canadian population, have not been able to penetrate into elite positions to the extent that their numbers might warrant. The elites are, hence, as 'unrepresentative' of the ethnic structure as they are of the class structure of the country as a whole. The degree of 'under-representation' varies from one sphere of activity to another, and within each social class there is an ethnic hierarchy.[12] The French, moreover, have their own hierarchies – the French Canadian labour elite, based in Quebec and Catholic in religion, the French-Catholic universities. The consequence, as Porter, as well as other Canadian commentators have pointed out, is not the 'melting-pot', which was the aim of US policy, but the 'mosaic' which is widely defended in Canada but which implies reduced social mobility and the continuance of segregation in the social and political structure. It can work, Porter suggests, as an instrument of social control by the British Canadian 'charter' group.[13]

The degree of 'representativeness' in the elite can therefore provide information about the distribution of opportunities within a society and about the likely extent of 'sponsored' rather than competitive upward mobility. Such study may even be able to predict the likelihood of anyone with a given background of having a range of political attitudes. It is unlikely to get any closer to an explanation of attitude and policy since there is no certainty that an aristocrat may not be a socialist or that a member of an under-privileged ethnic position will be a rebel rather than conform to the prevailing temper of the elite. For those who have gained elite status factors other than social background are often more important in determining policies and attitudes. Also significant are the need to gain political support from other groups, the experience of bargaining, the responsibilities of office. One might even hypothesise that those within the elite are likely to have transcended social, ethnic and class background in their ascent, whilst background factors typically exert a major influence on the attitudes of those who have remained in lower positions.

COMMUNITY POWER STUDIES

The difficulties of testing hypotheses as to the unity of the elite or elites at the head of society are very great indeed. Many of the difficulties are those of practicability. Any decisions taken at national level have a large number of ramifications. To study, as one must, a number of such decisions would be a protracted business and very expensive to carry out. It is doubtful whether the money can be raised to support a really detailed analysis. At the national level, moreover, access to decision-makers and the decision-making process is often very limited. Where access is not restricted, the political scientist is often prevented, on grounds of 'national interest', including in this term political embarrassment, or on grounds of official secrecy, from publishing his results and his sources of information in full. This renders very difficult the task of assessment and criticism by the academic world

and the public to whom the analyst is under an obligation to present his researches. To the extent that his work is 'censored' the student is in danger of offering an
apologia for the *status quo*.

This is not to say that studies of the activities, as distinct from the membership,
of elites at national level are foredoomed to failure. Remarkable successes have
been achieved. Nevertheless it seems fair to say that many national studies have
examined potential elites rather than proved the existence of actual elites who
have wielded a major or determining influence on a series of specific decisions.
The full information may not come to light until thirty years or more after the
event in question, although evidence is frequently forthcoming which will allow a
provisional if not a firmly established interpretation.

The need to formulate a researchable and publishable hypothesis within the
resources available has led many who have been interested in questions of decision-making to study smaller communities – city, town or village. Problems of
access can still be experienced at this level but they are less serious. However,
greater ease of access is often related to the decreased importance of the decisions
at issue, and it is still an unresolved question as to how far differences in scale constitute a difference in kind when examining decision-making. At the community
level one rarely finds issues of wide-ranging impact and of 'life-or-death' importance.[14] Despite these various difficulties community power studies have grown
apace in recent years. They have come to be the forum in which disputes about
power and elite relations take place especially in the USA. Two chief approaches
have been recommended – the reputational and the decision-making methods.
Both have been followed through with considerable imagination and thoroughness, and the disputes they have occasioned have become more than methodological. This has been a case in which arguments about method have become arguments about the nature of democratic political systems and, widest of all, arguments about the nature of politics itself.

(i) The 'reputational' approach
The reputational approach is mainly associated with Floyd Hunter's book
Community Power Structure.[15] Hunter's method comprised a number of stages,
each of which was designed to check on the previous stages. In the first stage
Hunter obtained preliminary lists of 'leaders' in 'Regional City' which were contributed by civic organisations, the Chamber of Commerce, the League of Women
Voters and by newspaper editors and 'other civic leaders'.[16] These lists named 175
leaders. The lists were partly derived from formal positions held in politics, businesses of a fairly large size and civic organisations. They were also partly based
on 'reputation' for leadership in the eyes of those who nominated them. The criteria for this preliminary selection thus vary in important respects.

The next stage was the selection of a panel of fourteen 'experts' or 'judges'
who were apparently 'representative' of religious, business and professional people. The panel balanced young and old, male and female, Negro and white. This
panel was asked to select the top leaders from each of the lists. The judges reduced

the leaders from 175 to forty. There was a fair degree of agreement amongst the judges as to the topmost men on each list. By this stage the attribution of power rests on the reputation of the leaders in the eyes of the judges. Hunter next interviewed twenty-seven of the forty leaders, who were asked to name the top ten leaders amongst the forty. Again there was a large measure of agreement. A range of supplementary questions elicited answers as to which leaders could push a decision through, and which one was 'the biggest man in town'. In order to discover the degree of cohesiveness amongst the leaders, each was asked how well he knew other leaders, whether he was related to them, how frequently he sat on committees with them.

These questions did uncover evidence which might support Mosca's contention that the minority as such is always better organised than the majority. The top leaders indicated that most of them knew one another well and that most had worked together on committees. Moreover, an inner group of twelve leaders nominated one another as friends, acquaintances and fellow committee members more frequently than the other leaders. There was a sharp drop in interaction among the leaders when the group of professional and civil workers immediately below the leadership was considered. This was taken to indicate a real gulf between the leadership stratum and the professional administrators. It seems reasonable to presume that there would be still less interaction between the leaders and the public at large. Hunter concluded from these researches that a clearly defined group of decision-makers dominated the public life of 'Regional City'. The leaders were not undivided but nevertheless it was their backing that was decisive to any major project.

At least half of Hunter's leaders were businessmen. Plural and interlocking directorships were common. Hunter interpreted such overlapping directorships to mean that there was a cohesive 'economic institution' in Regional City whose members exerted the major influence in the power relationships in the community.[17] These business leaders were discovered to be active in a number of policy decisions which Hunter examined, including the Plan of Development, traffic control and the introduction of a sales tax. The topmost leaders formulated 'big policy' on such questions, leaving the task of putting the policy through to, in the main, lesser figures who were either professionals, such as lawyers, or minor businessmen. Hunter regarded the top leaders in the committee as the representatives of the policymaking businessmen.

Hunter's conclusion was clearly that Regional City is ruled by a cohesive, conscious and conspiratorial elite of businessmen. The elite devises the major policy which the City will subsequently follow even though its members do not necessarily intervene overtly in the city's affairs. The elite has, according to Hunter, tentacles in most departments of Regional City's public life. The politicians of the legislature are themselves frequently businessmen who are controlled by or acknowledge the supremacy of the economic elite. In all, the 'economic institution' dominates and, as Hunter represents it, deputes specialists within it to oversee all the sectors of policy-making from the relation between city policy and national policy to the local matters of urban development and the sales tax.

Without necessarily doubting Hunter's conclusions concerning 'Regional City' many have adversely criticised the methods used in *Community Power Structure*. The two main criticisms have concerned the 'scope' of the decisions Hunter studied and the status of the expert 'judges' who provided the lists of reputed leaders. Followers of the rival 'decision-making' approach in particular have argued that, unlike their own method, Hunter's fails to distinguish the areas over which the several community leaders wield power. The original questions put to the judges asked them to nominate the persons who were the top leaders or decision-makers of the community. The judges were not asked to say over what spheres of activity each nominee exercised power nor what limits there might be to his influence, nor whether he might be powerful in some areas and not in others. Yet statements attributing power to a person may carry little meaning if the area of his power is not specified. Hunter did go on to study particular processes of decision-making and describe the elite's involvement in these. It has been less commonly noted that in these cases, however, Hunter investigated those issues which the members of the business elite had themselves cited as ones they had been interested in.[18] Such a procedure is circular since it merely measures the degree of involvement of the elite in matters which it has already asserted it was involved in. These were very clearly issues which affected business interests. On non-economic issues the leaders are shown to be divided and unwilling or unable to offer a lead.[19] It is thus a possibility that outside matters affecting business another set of leaders may be more influential.

The reputational method is clearly heavily dependent on its selection of judges at the outset, and it has been a constant criticism that some alternative sample of judges might have set the inquiry on a totally different course. Several articles have discovered that there is a very significant difference between the nominations of judges who are active in the community and of those who participate very little. The politically active 'judges' are more likely than the inactive to nominate men from 'behind the scenes' rather than those in leading public positions. Other researchers have, however, found that varying the nominating panel made little difference to the results.[20] This is not to say that either way of designating leaders is necessarily wrong. It does, however, point to the substantive differences which can arise as a result of the adoption of different research procedures.

Hunter's method of continually narrowing down the number of leaders at each stage of interviewing may also appear self-confirming. He began with a provisional list of nominees. He then asked fourteen judges to select the most influential from the original list of 175. Hunter proceeded to a closer examination of the top forty in the judges' reduced list although there seems, as Polsby points out,[21] no clear account as to how the figure forty is arrived at. At the interviewing stage only twenty-seven of this forty were questioned, and the subsequent estimates made by the leadership group of the comparative influence of each leader is based on these twenty-seven interviews. It is again not clear why only twenty-seven were interviewed, nor what the criteria of selection were. Finally, although those interviewed named sixty-four additional persons as being as influential as the forty nominees[22] these sixty-four are not examined in further detail.

(ii) The 'decision-making' approach

Robert A. Dahl's work, in particular *Who Governs?*,[23] is the outstanding example of the decision-making approach. His stated purpose is to test a number of hypotheses that have been put forward concerning who governs in a modern democracy. The elitist interpretation, to which Dahl devotes most of his attention, he defines as the view that power is concentrated as a result of the inequalities in the distribution of resources of influence in the community. Power will be held by those who hold the greatest wealth, the highest social status or some crucial business position. Dahl points out that politicians play little part in decision-making on such interpretations – a point borne out by Floyd Hunter's book.

Dahl held that the only way to test such assertions would be to examine in detail some significant political decisions in a community. The decisions selected would need to be varied in their content so as to check whether one group made decisions in many aspects of a community's affairs rather than only in one. Examining a series of decisions should also reveal how far the decision-makers operate as a conscious, cohesive and conspiratorial group and how far their power is 'cumulative', their political power stemming from their wealth and status. Dahl also gave a historical dimension to his inquiry by attempting a survey of New Haven society politics from the eighteenth century to the 1950s in an attempt to show how the power structure had changed in response to changes in society. A report on decision-making in New Haven could not necessarily imply that all other communities would display an identical pattern of decision-making. The city could, however, be regarded as fairly typical of American communities in its varied distribution of political resources, the equality of voting rights being balanced by the enormous inequalities in property holding.

Dahl selected three distinct 'issue-areas' for analysis which would clearly test the range of any hypothetical elite's influence. These were decisions on urban redevelopment, decisions on public schools and decisions on political nominations, particularly for the post of mayor. Within each issue area a number of decisions were studied. As in the case of Floyd Hunter's investigation these decisions were the ones regarded by the participants themselves as the most important. This again might give rise to the criticism that policies which the leaders did not regard as important, but which the mass of the community believed important, would be disregarded in the investigation.[24]

Dahl also distinguished three categories of potential leaders – politicians (holders of certain elective offices), 'social notables' and 'economic notables'. The intention was to study whether each category participated in decisions in any or all of the three issue areas. Dahl took as signs of influence the frequency with which a person initiates important policy against opposition or is able to exercise a veto over policies initiated by others, or initiates policy which does not meet with opposition.[25] If public office were distributed randomly then the social notables held more public offices than might be anticipated on the basis of the small numbers involved. Even so, the proportion of offices held by the members of 'high society' was small. Nor did many exercise real influence by initiating or vetoing policies.[26] Social notables were seldom at the same time economic notables. Men of established families went into the professions rather than business, the leading positions in which were occupied by men from out of town or of lower social origin.

The economic notables were more active. Their activities were largely directed to questions of urban development, the single issue area which closely affected their interests. No economic notable held office relating to public education and few held a party office, largely because few lived in New Haven itself, which was a condition of office in these matters. This fact does suggest that the choice of these two issue areas to test the elitist hypothesis was unfortunate. The economic leaders of New Haven undoubtedly started with considerable political advantages. They possessed wealth, a certain status, authority on business and finance, the advantages of communication accruing to minorities and the legitimacy which attaches to business itself in America though not in many other societies.[27] Such resources in themselves, however, make the business leaders only a potential and not, as yet, an actual elite. Dahl's conclusion was that the resources were never effectively used. The economic notables were divided amongst themselves even on urban development, in which the elected mayor took the initiative. Their activity was confined only to one of the issue areas examined, and their small numbers meant that their votes did not count for much at election time.

From the very comprehensive data he was able to collect Dahl felt able to reconstruct in considerable detail the key decisions in the three issue-areas between 1950–59 (in the case of political nominations the period covered from 1941–57). The reconstruction was, of course, by outside observers. Nevertheless *Who Governs?* describes the decision-making process in large part through the eyes of the major participants. Dahl then fits these varied and competing perspectives into a pattern which could not have been perceived in its entirety by any of the decision-makers. He recounts how the problems appeared to the participants, what they believed to be the attitudes of supporters and opponents, what they saw as alternatives and how they interpreted their own policy initiatives.

A major point upon which Dahl insists is that the interpretations that activists make of the political reactions of others is an extremely important factor in prompting their own responses and is, consequently, a factor essential to any analysis of political events. It was the New Haven Mayor's interpretation – correct or incorrect – of his electoral victory that prompted him to campaign more strongly for the urban redevelopment programme. The student, Dahl and his associates argue, can only start from the subjective evaluations of policy alternatives of the participants and should not interpolate his own account of the alternatives 'objectively' open to them. In consequence Dahl's study is of the agenda for decision as it is seen by the decision-makers themselves.[28]

The evidence Dahl collected suggested that the structure of decision making in

New Haven could be described as a form of pluralism. It approximates to what Dahl has elsewhere termed a 'polyarchy'. In a polyarchy the population is divided into a large number of minority groups which may in some cases be exclusive and in other cases may overlap. In an idealised version of a polyarchy all such groups would possess equal information about possible policies, equal political resources to influence outcomes, equal opportunity to participate politically by putting forward claims which all would do as occasion arose.[29] Not all these equalities, however, will be found in any empirical community.[30] There are no political systems in which political resources are equally distributed. Invariably some sections of a population have more resources and more influence than others. The ways in which the resources are distributed will also vary from one society to another. In one country the chief political resource may be wealth, in another race, in yet another education.

Whereas elitists see the control of such resources as always cumulative Dahl does not believe this to be true of polyarchies. Wealth does not necessarily give rise to political power nor social status to economic power – a point borne out in Dahl's New Haven studies. Despite inequalities in the possession of resources no group in a polyarchy is totally lacking in them. At the very minimum each minority group has its voting strength since it is a condition of a polyarchy that no one is by law denied the right to vote. Beyond this it may have the wealth to publicise its own views or to put up its own political candidates or possess the threat to withdraw its labour in the event of its own policy being rejected. Such 'liberal democratic' rights and freedoms are again basic to polyarchal systems. Moreover, though there may be inequalities in the distribution of resources a minority with greater potential influence may, just like a person, be less efficient or less active in its use of the resources than one with fewer at its disposal.

Society in a polyarchy, then, contains a large number of minority groups equipped with a variety of political resources which are unequally distributed between them, and which are used with varying degrees of intensity and efficiency. Each member of the community possesses equal political rights. Only a small proportion of the members of each group, however, is politically active. The leadership may be elected by the group itself, as in the case of leaders of trade unions. It may result from the lack of interest of the bulk of the group in participating directly to further group aims. The consequence is that social decision-making is in the hands of a number of elites, though Dahl would not call them such presumably because the leadership sub-group is not closed to outsiders and does not necessarily exercise a veto-power over the members of its own minority. Many of these minority leaders, such as union leaders, hold positions of influence over long periods. Others are replaced at frequent intervals. Some leading activists in New Haven intervened in public affairs for the first time in their lives when a matter affecting themselves directly arose, proved successful, and were drawn into the public world to serve regularly on committees. Others intervened in the defence of their interests but, despite the success of their campaign, retired once again into the private realm. All such leaders remained specialists in their own issue areas.

The politicians in a polyarchy are themselves a minority divided into two or more rival parties competing for public office which is achieved by obtaining a majority of votes at an election. In a polyarchy this means building a policy platform which will appeal to a plurality of the minorities in the society. Certain minorities may be firmly attached to one party camp rather than another. A significant number, however, is prepared to shift its allegiance in response to a party's promised policies. As a result no political leader can afford for very long to ignore the claims of any substantial minority lest it add its weight to give a plurality to his opponent. He, and his opponents, will tend to moderate their policies, avoid ideological positions or points of principle, in order to gain the support of the most marginal minorities. The ultimate objective of all political parties is to construct a set of policies which will satisfy the largest number of minorities – represented by their leaderships – in the electoral market place. It will be the closest approximation to a consensus.

Equal political participation does not exist in the polyarchy but nor is there a single elite. Minorities and their leaders will tend to be specialists in their own issue areas. The politicians who aim at the positions which will give them the overall view of the battle are themselves dependent on the support of the many authorities. Should they construct a set of policies which did not satisfy a plurality of minorities at the elections they would be thrown out of office. The vast majority of the population participates very little in politics but Dahl does not recognise this majority as the inert and ineffective mass of elitist theory. The peoples' influence is indirect through their potential voting strength, and the estimates the politicians make of the electorate's likely future use of that strength which causes them to modify and withdraw policies and replace them by others more appealing.

The picture of 'decision-makers' confined in the main to a particular issue area and responsive to the attitudes and pressures of others leaves a highly atomised picture of polyarchal decision-making which Dahl, despite his adherence to pluralism, corrects to some extent. The picture so far given does not show how the several men of influence settle conflicts or develop some agreement on priorities. Dahl tested a number of hypotheses as to how the policies might be integrated, and discovered several patterns of integration to have existed in New Haven.[31] Such patterns of integration may appear to accentuate the division between leaders and led. But it is Dahl's contention that all such patterns involve skill in bargaining rather than the conscious, conspiratorial use of veto power characteristic of an elite. In particular all such leaders are aware of their dependence on electoral mood. It is this awareness, Dahl believes, that will ensure that the claims put forward by every minority will at least be heard by the leaders, even though nothing can of course ensure that all claims will be accepted and acted upon. How far such conclusions are the products of the research methods used and the assumptions held must await examination in the following chapter.

(iii) Works of synthesis
Since the publication of the works of Hunter and of Dahl a number of communi-

ty studies have appeared which have clearly benefited from the advances that Hunter and Dahl each made, and also from the extensive criticism which has been levelled against these pioneers. The more recent works on community power have sought to incorporate the rival methodologies, reputational and decision-making, to provide a more comprehensive account of the influences affecting community decisions. Among the most thorough of such works of synthesis are Robert Agger and others, *The Rulers and the Ruled*,[32] a comparative study of two communities in the western and two in the southern USA, and Robert Presthus, *Men at the Top*,[33] which is a study of two small communities in New York State.[34]

A prime aim of both Agger and Presthus was to examine the images that citizens had of the power structure which were likely to affect the nature and extent of their political participation. It is a highly significant matter whether the power structure appears open to any citizen who makes some effort to participate and whether the men of influence are likely to be interested in the particular community problems which seem important to that citizen. The 'image' of the power structure is a factor which any political elite will take into account in assessing its own influence and freedom of action. The mutual assessments of elite and citizenry or 'mass' is consequently a factor which the student of elites must also weigh in his conclusions. It is, however, a factor which many critics claim is ignored in the decision-making approach which concentrates on the part individuals and sets of leaders play in specific decisions, and omits to assess the ideological framework within which the decision is reached.

Agger discovered potential leaders by asking two independent panels, drawn from leaders of voluntary organisations and appointed officials in local government, to nominate the men of greatest influence in the community, the second panel being requested to reduce the nominees to around twenty five.[35] The decisions selected for study were in part chosen by the panels and in part by the authors. The nominees were interviewed to discover the nature of their participation, their attitude to the various decisions reached, and their views of the roles of other participants, in particular whether leadership cliques were formed. Finally, Agger reconstructed the history of each decision to test whether the potential leaders had actually participated, especially at the crucial stage at which the project is accepted or rejected. This decision-making approach also established whether the leaders specialised in issue areas, as Dahl had suggested, or were 'generalists' such as Hunter had discovered in 'Regional City'.

Agger's conclusions are too vast and detailed for ready summary. A major point, however, is that the communities vary considerably in their power structures, some being pluralist and others elitist in tendency. Whether or not the reputation and decision-making approaches in isolation led inevitably to elitist and pluralist conclusions respectively it would seem that, used in combination, they constituted a neutral methodology capable of a variety of results.

Presthus came to this same conclusion from his application of both techniques in *Men at the Top*. Here the two methods were explicitly used as checks upon one another. Presthus admits an original preference for the decisional approach as more 'objective' but rapidly discovered that the reputation method led in directions which the case study of decisions could not cover. The decisional approach, Presthus held, over-emphasised the importance of those in formal positions of power, in particular the political leaders. In one of the communities studied a man who participated in four out of five different decisions was, nevertheless, not nominated as an 'influential' either by the sample of citizens interviewed or by the other influential. The disparity in the conclusions of the two methods pointed to the fact that this person played only a 'ministerial' role in implementing the various decisions but was not an initiator of projects. Similarly a leader might appear to be a major participant in a range of decisions simply because his post formally required his *imprimatur* on policy conclusions already arrived at by others.

Conversely the decision-making approach may fail to mention persons nominated in the reputational lists. This may deflate the importance of the reputational nominations. It may show that not all those with the resources to exercise power, whom the reputation approach mostly lists, do in fact exercise power. Such men may, as Dahl painted out, simply lack the time or the interest to participate, or may have a distaste for the political arena, as both Dahl and Presthus discovered to be true of many economic leaders. On the other hand, when, as Presthus found, men who have been proved to be decision-makers nevertheless nominate as influential other persons not identified as important by studies of any actual decision it would seem worth while looking behind the formal decision. As a result Presthus discovered men of considerable influence, usually arising from their wealth, their formal positions in such institutions as banks or their social prestige and connections, who did not directly participate in a single decision. Their influence was evidenced in a number of ways. Other decision-makers and influentials acknowledged that they had consulted X prior to initiating a project. Ascertaining his views as to the feasibility and desirability of a policy was thought necessary before putting it forward to other influentials or to the public. Where funds were to be raised his backing was advisable and he was inevitably one of the first to be approached. In 'Edgewood' one such influential named Wainwright, a public-spirited person, head of a family-owned corporation, with a long record of quiet service to the community, influenced the financing of a new hospital by pitching his contribution early enough and at such a level as to ensure high contributions from others. It was particularly at the 'take-off' stage of a programme that such figures played their crucial roles. But Wainwright never allowed himself to be directly involved in the battles over the project or in pushing it through. Wainwright and other such individuals were found, tacitly or explicitly, to depute others, usually an employee, to take a direct part in the decision-making. Such 'leg-men', also discovered by Hunter, were identified by the decisional method but were seldom nominated as influentials by the reputation method.

Such 'behind-the-scenes' influence does not in this instance indicate any covert conspiracy. It is, however, clearly a very significant factor in influencing the course of events in the community. The combination of the two methods permitted Presthus to identify both the public and private stages of decision-making in a scientific manner without falling into the error, pointed out by Dahl on many occasions, of always presuming that there is a further covert clique behind each set of decision-makers uncovered.

Presthus reported that there was, however, a considerable disparity between those identified by the reputation and decisional methods. In part this was due to the recognised failings of the reputation method. It tended to identify as actually powerful those whose resources gave them a high potential for power. Respondents also nominated as influential those they felt 'should' be influential, especially those in their own party, and minimised the role of their opponents. For these reasons Presthus was unable to commend the reputation method for use in isolation, but he found the complementary use of both devices led to a deeper understanding of the variety of ways in which influence is exercised.

One of the aims of Presthus's study was to construct an elitist-pluralist continuum on which to place communities and provide a means of ready comparison between them. To achieve this required not only the examination of overlapping decision-making amongst the leaders. It also needed research into the degree of individual citizen participation in major decisions, the extent to which citizens joined voluntary organisation and how far these organisations were themselves involved in decision-making. Presthus found that both his communities were more elitist than New Haven as portrayed by Dahl, but that 'Edgewood' was less elitist than 'Riverview'. In 'Edgewood' decision-making was shared between the economic notables and the politicians with the economic elite dominant. In 'Riverview', two politicians held the initiative. Presthus, like Agger, thereby emphasises the diversity of power structures and challenges any implication by either Hunter or Dahl that elitism or pluralism is ubiquitous.

Citizen participation, whether direct or indirect, was low in both communities. The study confirmed the findings of a good deal of other research that individual 'rank-and-file' participation in decision-making is minimal. Only 10 per cent of the 'Riverview' population and 26 per cent of those in 'Edgewood' took any part in any decision-making, these figures moreover being inflated by the numbers who merely voted in referenda. The bulk of the population in both communities did not belong to any voluntary organisation and though 52 per cent of 'Edgewood' and 25 per cent of 'Riverview' organisations participated in decisions they were very seldom involved in more than one issue area. The vast majority of citizens are therefore non-participants, and the organisations do not in fact perform the linking function which pluralists claim they perform or ought to perform.

To explain this situation Presthus turned, as did both Agger and Rose, to the citizens' perceptions of the political system, the ideological dimension not adequately covered by the decisional approach. Elitism was found to go hand in hand with political 'alienation' defined as a sense of political ineffectiveness which results in withdrawal from the public realm. Whereas the leaderships of both communities remained overwhelmingly convinced that anyone in the town who wanted to have his say in important matters could have it, the citizenry was generally more sceptical, and a substantial minority believed this and similar assertions to be false. In general such alienation was found to be correlated with low class status, and more limited education. A sense of political effectiveness is clearly a stimulus to participation. When such a sense is lost in the face of a real or imagined elitism there is a tendency to withdraw from politics which only goes to further confirm the elitist structure. Political inertia on the part of a population cannot therefore be taken as a sign of satisfaction with the leadership.[36]

CONCLUSION

As stated at the outset of the chapter, the task students of elites have to face is to establish the degree to which any leadership group is cohesive, conscious and conspiratorial. The recent empirical studies of 'manageable' communities have produced more reliable techniques for measuring these factors. This appears particularly true of the work of those like Agger and Presthus who, with apparent eclecticism, incorporate contrasting methods to use them as tests upon one another and upon the empirical material uncovered. They have taken the important step, which is likely to be further pursued, of comparing the characteristics of the so-called 'mass' with those of the supposed elite in order to examine the contrast, alleged so vigorously by elitists, in their activism, capacities for initiative, apathy, education and social status. No doubt such studies will be further refined, but there yet remains the problem of interpreting the results of such inquiries. At what point on the continuum, and for what reasons, does the interpreter decide to term a society pluralist rather than elitist? Is it enough that a society is ruled by competing elites or should it display a considerable degree of individual political participation? In the next chapter some further methodological and substantive problems of both elitism and pluralism will be examined.

NOTES

1   Sampson, *Anatomy of Britain*, p. 347.

2   See Paul Ferris, *The City*, Penguin Books, Harmondsworth, 1962, especially pp. 63–6.

3   *Winchester and the Public School Elite*, Faber, London, 1967, pp. 26–8.

4   See the 'family trees' in Sampson, *Anatomy of Britain Today*, Hodder and Stoughton, London, 1965, pp. 411 and 434.

5   T. Lupton and C. S. Wilson, 'The Social Background and Connections of 'Top Decision Makers'', *Manchester School*, XXVII, 1959, pp. 30–51.

6   Paul Ferris, *The City*, p. 141.

7   See C. H. Dodd, 'Recruitment to the Administrative Class, 1960–64', *Public Administration*, Spring, 1967, p. 59 and *passim*.

8   See L. J. Edinger and D. D. Searing, 'Social Background in Elite Analysis', *American Political Science Review*, LXI, 2, 1967, pp. 428–45; G. A. Almond and S. Verba, *The Civic*

Culture, Little, Brown, Boston and Toronto, 1965.

9 J. Blondel, *Voters, Parties and Leaders*, 1963, pp. 10–11 and *passim*.

10 More strictly, a 'ruling class', since it is composed of the majority of the society.

11 *The Vertical Mosaic*, University of Toronto Press, Toronto, 1965.

12 Porter, *The Vertical Mosaic*, pp. 286–7, 387–9, 441–2, 76–90.

13 Porter, pp. 70-3. Ch. III discusses 'Ethnicity and Social Class' with great thoroughness.

14 See further below, pp. 116–8, on 'boundary' problems.

15 University of North Carolina Press, 1953; references will be to the edition by Anchor Books, Garden City, New York, 1963.

16 Hunter, pp. 62 and 261.

17 Hunter, 1963, pp. 81-2.

18 Hunter, p. 222.

19 Hunter, pp. 217 ff.

20 On these issues see articles by R.O. Schulze and L.U. Blumberg, 'The Determination of Local Power Elites', *American Journal of Sociology*, Nov. 1957, pp. 290–6; G. Belknap and R. Smuckler, 'Political Power Relations in a Mid-West City', *Public Opinion Quarterly*, Spring 1956, pp. 73–81.

21 Nelson W. Polsby, *Community Power and Political Theory*, Yale, U.P. 1963, pp. 48–9.

22 Hunter, *Community Power Structure*, p. 65.

23 Yale University Press, New Haven, 1961.

24 A possibility further discussed below in Chapter V.

25 Dahl, *Who Governs?*, p. 66.

26 Dahl, *Who Governs?*, pp. 64–6.

27 Dahl, *Who Governs?*, pp. 75–6.

28 See below, pp. 108–13, for a further discussion of the problems of interpretation this raises.

29 Dahl, *A Preface to Democratic Theory*, Phoenix edition, Chicago, 1963, Ch.3.

30 Dahl, *Modern Political Analysis*, 1963, pp. 32–7.

31 Dahl, *Who Governs?*, pp. 184 ff.

32 R. Agger, D. Goldrich and B. Swanson, *The Rulers and the Ruled*, Wiley, New York, 1964. Henceforth referred to as Agger.

33 Oxford University Press, New York, 1964.

34 Also relevant is Arnold M. Rose, *The Power Structure*, Oxford University Press, Galaxy Books, New York, 1967, which is more concerned with national elites, though it does discuss the power relationships of communities in Minnesota.

35 Agger outlines the method briefly on pp. 707 ff.

36 See the further discussion below, pp. 108–13.

chapter five | criticisms of the elite concept

The survey given in the previous chapters of the work of elitists and pluralists has described a direct conflict about research methodology as well as about the substantive conclusions reached. The concluding chapter will suggest that these disputes have become arguments about political ideology. Empirical work on elites has come to revive a very ancient debate as to the proper role of leadership in a democracy. It is a debate as old as political theory itself, as the writings of Plato and Aristotle witness.

The disputes among elitists and pluralists have been fruitful: they have sharpened the ideological arguments and refined many of the important concepts of political science. This chapter will examine critically some of the attempts by both elitists and pluralists to provide more precise accounts of the central terms of political science. It will look in particular at the nature of political power and influence, at the grounds on which such power can be attributed to persons and groups, and at the problems of explaining 'decision-making'. Neither pluralists nor elitists have been totally convincing on these issues. In part this has been the consequence of their methodologies and in part it has resulted from the assumptions with which they have begun or the inferences which they have drawn from their material.

THE SCOPE OF INFLUENCE

Robert A. Dahl and his research associate in the New Haven project, Nelson W. Polsby, can be regarded as the leading representatives of the modern pluralistic approach. Their crucial criticism of elitists is that they have failed to define the 'scope' of the influence wielded by members of the elite. Dahl's point is simple but at the same time acute: to assert that a person has power or influence is meaningless unless it is specified which realms of activities he is able to influence.[1] A person may influence transport policy but not agricultural policy. His influence may thus be confined to a single 'issue area' or he may exercise a more general influence over a number of areas. Furthermore influence in any area should be measured for size and intensity. The numbers influenced need to be estimated as well as the degree of effort needed to persuade them from their original intentions. Some persons and groups will be more hostile to moving in a new direction than will others. The person able to move such men may be thought more influential than those who can convert the more fickle. For such reasons a government may include in its ranks individuals who have special influence over participants in particular areas, such as over unions or over private employers.

Elitists, believing power to be cumulative, have tended to regard all influentials as 'generalists' who exercise power in all matters. They speak of elite 'power' as such, giving the impression of a monolithic, undifferentiated entity in the hands of the few. This error is to be found in elitist writings from Mosca to Hunter. C. Wright Mills provides examples in *The Power Elite*, despite having in another work, *The Sociological Imagination*, recorded research notes which outline a project which promised interesting results but which, unfortunately, he failed to carry out:[2]

> Project: select 3 or 4 key decisions of last decade – to drop the atom, to cut or raise steel production, the G.M. strike of '45 – and trace in detail the personnel involved in each of them.

Such a project would cover a range of decisions in markedly different issue areas. If Mills had discovered the same persons making decisions or wielding great influence in all these areas he would have gone a long way towards establishing the existence of his power elite. In fact *The Power Elite* looked only, and then not in detail, at 'big' decisions in the field of foreign policy – Hiroshima, Korea, Quemoy and Matsu, Dien bien phu. Moreover, this selection of decisions is highly tendentious since they all very obviously involve at least two sections of Mills's power elite – the military and the political executive, though even here he makes scarcely a reference to the role of the President. There is no attempt to show how the military elite was involved in the strike of automobile workers or in a decision affecting social welfare.

Dahl, as has been noted previously, did examine participants in differing issue areas and found scarcely any overlap in New Haven, although others, like Presthus, using similar techniques, have found stronger tendencies towards elitism in other communities. Dahl's distinction between economic notables, social notables and political leaders mirrors the common distinction between wealth, status and power. The pluralist case that there is not necessarily a high correlation between the hierarchies of wealth, status and power and that consequently they are not to be *presumed* to be cumulative resources, must be accepted as correct. This cannot, of course, prove that they might not be connected in particular instances, that New Haven might represent one relationship and 'Regional City' another. Moreover, the distinction between wealth, status and power, though important, can be misleading. Recognising that wealth and power are empirically separable variables in assessing a person's or a group's resources, it is nevertheless the case that an individual or a group which controls another's economic life-chances is exercising some degree of power.

A powerful man is not necessarily wealthy, a wealthy man not necessarily powerful. But wealth often goes along with the control of economic resources, direction of an industry, control of investment funds, determination of wages and prices. These can very often be used in such a way as to reduce another's life chances by refusing him credit for his business, rejecting a wage claim, hiring him or firing him and so on. The life-chances of the wealthy man and the poor man must be counted as resources which either can use to influence his situation. They are in this sense 'powers' defined as "present means to some future apparent good". Polsby, in his understandable desire to refute the elitist claim that a connection invariably exists between high economic position and political power, appears not to recognise that power can arise from the use to which wealth is put.[3] His over-sharp distinction between wealth and power appears to rule out the possible existence of a ruling elite of economic dominants by definition. Polsby, so alert to the errors of the earlier elitists in community power research, in this instance commits the mistake of which he accuses his adversaries. His pluralist conclusions are embedded in pluralist definitions.

Analogous to the fallacy of aggregating different scopes of influence to constitute a single undifferentiated sphere of power is the fallacy of aggregating the different ways in which influence has been wielded in a given issue area by elites in the past and presuming that all these methods of influence are available at any time to any elite operating in this sphere of activity. S. E. Finer exposes the fallacy in his study of 'The Political Power of Private Capital'.[4] He points out that the fact that business is able to exert one kind of influence in one particular country or at one particular period does not permit the leap to asserting that business can exert the same influence in another country or at another point in time. The use of bribery by business in one country, the use of physical coercion to break up strikes in another country, of a 'crisis of confidence' to undermine the government in yet another country, do not add up to 'the political power' of business as such a power available at the fingertips of the business elite at any time and place.

Such a fallacy may seem too obvious to deceive anybody. It is, however, not unusual amongst elitists. 'Classical' elitists such as Mosca, Pareto and Burnham commit it regularly in their highly selective appeals to historical evidence in support of their sociological laws. Instances of the powers of rulers are taken from widely differing societies and periods in order to verify the inevitable existence of an elite with a monopoly of 'power'. At best such aggregations of powers could be regarded as an 'ideal type' of power to which an elite will approximate, or aspire, but which is very unlikely to be possessed by any empirical elite.

All these criticisms of the failure of elitists to define the scope of a given group's influence lead up to a further distinction which Dahl and other pluralists have insisted upon. This is the distinction between potential and actual power or influence.[5] Mills amongst elitists does partially recognise this when pointing out that those who hold the pivotal positions in society do not necessarily make use of them to determine the course of events. To list a person's resources does not necessarily identify him as a man of influence. As has been shown in many community studies, an individual or a group has to possess interest, determination and skill before committing resources to action. Someone with fewer total resources may use them with greater enthusiasm and imagination than someone with far greater potential power. Again, however, this distinction between potential and actual influence is not as clear-cut as pluralists sometimes claim. Even where a person or group with potential for power does not actually exercise it, others may believe him to exercise it, or be about to exercise it. Such estimates may be mistaken but they can nevertheless influence the actions of those making them to the extent of leading them to modify or withdraw their proposals. This, without the holder of the resources lifting a finger or even intending to do so.[6]

POLITICAL INFLUENCE: APPEARANCE AND REALITY

It is as important for the understanding of a society to study the perceptions or 'images' its members have of the society's power structure as it is to study the way in which the structure works 'in fact'. Indeed, 'fact' and 'image' are often very difficult to disentangle. Elitists (and Marxists) have paid a good deal of attention to this in their analyses of ideology. Systems of ideas which further the interests of the elite become, elitists argue, part of the values of the ordinary citizen and organise his perceptions of the political system in a manner which helps reinforce the elite's dominance. The converse, however, is equally possible. The power structure of a society may not appear to the man-in-the-street in the same favourable light that it does to the elite. Such differences in reaction have to be taken into account by students of political influence since they can have a considerable effect upon the nature of the relationships between the decision-makers and the rest of the society. Pluralists, with the notable exception of Joseph A. Schumpeter,[7] have in recent years paid rather less attention than the elitists to the role of ideologies and images in influencing power relations. Voting studies have, admittedly, examined the sense of political efficacy amongst voters and its connection with political participation, but they have rarely gone deeply into its consequences for the power structure of societies.

One of the major claims made by Dahl and his associates on behalf of polyarchies is that under them the interests of the various segments of society receive attention from the leaderships. In a competitive political situation the interest of the political leaders in re-election will ensure that the various interests of society will be considered lest any of these minority interests casts its vote for the opponents. As Polsby puts it,[8] "In the decision-making of fragmented government...the claims of small intense minorities are usually attended to". The implication is that any minority can gain a degree of satisfaction by using the established democratic procedures to put forward its claims. This does not, of course, mean that all their claims will be acceded to but they will at least be considered. This makes it 'unnecessary' and 'inefficient' for any group to attempt to mobilise large-scale class or mass participation to bring pressure upon the leaderships when its interests are pressed and satisfied in piecemeal fashion by the ordinary democratic procedures.[9]

This analysis again ignores the perceptions of those in the community who are not closely involved in the decision-making process. It is not a necessary truth that in a competitive political situation all interests will be considered, let alone accommodated. A comparison can be made with a competitive market situation in economics. Such a market can only claim to meet the effective *demands* of the consumers, i.e. demands backed by purchasing power. It does not attend to the *needs* of everyone in the community since not all needs may be backed by purchasing power, and such needs do not go forward as demands. The competitive market may continue to satisfy demands without being concerned with the level of needs.

It is possible for a similar situation to arise in competitive politics. Political 'interests' can be regarded as equivalent to 'needs' and 'claims' as corresponding to 'demands'. Competing political leaders, without being in any way in collusion, might not take into account the interests as distinct from the claims of one or more minorities. In such a situation certain policy options will not be dealt with by the decision makers. These options will not, moreover, come to light in research adopting the decisional method which can look only at overt issues arising from claims which have appeared in the political market place and been considered by the political leaders.

Dahl's polyarchy is not in fact the only political system compatible with competitive politics. In the first place it can be noted that polyarchy is not to be identified with what has in the past been termed 'democratic pluralism'. Pluralism has meant a system in which power is shared between the state and the maximum possible number of groups and individuals. A very high degree of participation is anticipated, from voting and attending meetings to seeking public office and taking part in the process of decision-making. Such pluralism will regard a high degree of individual participation as an ideal.[10] By contrast modern pluralism, of which the polyarchal theory is an outstanding instance, will regard a polity as pluralist provided there is competition between a few elites. The population at large is represented by the elites of the competing organisations which all members of the society are free to enter if they wish. Polyarchy is pluralism suited to an age of organisation. It is this system, not 'classical' pluralism, which Dahl found existing in New Haven and which he and Polsby seem to regard as the likely outcome of political competition.

Apart from 'classical' pluralism and polyarchy, other situations can arise within a competitive context as a consequence of the perceptions, attitudes or ideologies of the participants. A third possibility is that claims may be put forward by minorities but may not be considered by any of the competing leadership groups. There may arise a gulf between the competing leaders and one minority group whose support is not courted because it may alienate the support of a number of other groups. Minorities advocating public amenities such as concert halls and theatres may find themselves in such a position when their projects seem to the politicians to be too costly in money terms and not profitable enough in terms of the votes to be gained, in much the same way as such public projects can often not be financed on the market where no entrepreneur can see a profit for himself. Advocates of very radical programmes may find themselves similarly ignored. Even substantial minorities may experience the same frustration. There is evidence that the large Negro minority in the USA could be one such group. Both the studies by Hunter and by Agger, Goldrich and Swanson found that in some communities there was a considerable disparity between how the Negro activists and the White leaders ranked issues in order of importance to the community.[11] To the Negroes slum clearance and housing were the chief issues, whilst the Whites were very little concerned with these issues.

It is this apparent inability on the part of some minorities to have their claims put on the agenda for public decision that can give rise to a fourth possible situation occurring within the competitive system. The frustrated minority might cease to put forward claims for public consideration even though its interest in, say, housing improvements certainly persists. Two consequences might follow from this withdrawal from the ordinary democratic procedures.

Firstly, the minority might become apathetic, believing participation to be fruitless. Their interests would not appear as demands for the political leaders to consider or for the researchers into community decisions to describe. Both leaders and researchers might readily conclude that absence of demands is indicative of the minority's satisfaction, whereas it indicates the minority's alienation from the political system. According to surveys in the USA alienation, measured in terms of a sense of political inefficacy, appears to be associated with low positions on the scale of social classes. Those concerned tend to belong to fewer organisations and many belong to none. Consequently, they are in a relatively poor position to translate their very real needs and interests into claims, particularly if there is no large class-based party to represent them.

Secondly, this quiescent withdrawal may give way to the mass intervention inside or outside the established political system which pluralists hold to be unnecessary and inefficient. Polyarchal pluralism appears to imply that claims put forward by the competing elites comprehend the needs and interests of society. Democracy can therefore function smoothly through the bargaining of the elites and does not require the high degree of participation which traditional political theory has held to be essential to a true democracy. However, dissident minorities fearing a consensus of opinion amongst the otherwise competing elites which will result in their interests not being considered may resort to massive protest movements, non-violent demonstrations or violence itself in order to break the consensus and have their arguments placed on the agenda. In the 1960s the USA in particular has witnessed movements which could be interpreted in this way, such as those over civil rights and Vietnam and the violent Negro protests in the cities. If some of these issues might be said to be on the agenda already they either had low priority or else some of the possible policy alternatives had been implicitly ruled out by the leaders despite their need to compete for support.

Such violent reactions against the regime often puzzle those participating in it to whom the system appears open to any influence which organises itself in a legitimate manner. The definition of 'legitimate' in such a context will itself involve excluding some ways of exerting pressure and can exclude certain policies as well, particularly where they threaten the political system itself. In the cases of alienated revolt, however, the 'fact', if such can be established, that a regime is open to any pressure is less important than the perceptions of those affected by it. To a frustrated minority a polyarchy may appear to be a power elite imposing its policy with the full coercive backing available to the community's governors. There is some evidence that this is how many Negroes have interpreted the American political system. Injunctions to test the system by campaigning through organisations to influence the leadership in the polyarchal fashion may fall on deaf ears if the minority has, or believes itself to have, long been denied a proper hearing.

Both elitists and pluralists have, for their very different reasons, held that a consensus as to the values of a political system is important to its survival. A system, it is widely argued, could not persist long in the same form if either its leaders or the bulk of the population abandoned the ideology which supported it – denied the divinity of kingship in sixteenth and seventeenth century monarchies, or the right of free elections in modern western democracies. It has frequently been suggested that a high degree of consensus amongst leaders can result in a democracy approaching or appearing to approach an elitist form of rule. The existence of a broad agreement on social values throughout a nation can raise difficult problems for understanding its power structure.

As a general rule studies of the exercise of political power concentrate on disputes between politicians or between the leaders and their publics. This has the drawback of ignoring the habits of a society both in its practices and its ways of thinking. The case-study of decision making is particularly prone to this error. Presthus admits that his sample of decisions could not be termed strictly 'representative' since they were too important to be very frequent and hence they aroused greater interest and participation by the powerful. Edward C. Banfield, in *Political Influence*,[12] a particularly interesting example of the decisional approach applied to a large city, argues that the exercise of influence occurs where there is controversy and that the non-controversial is of little interest. In 'steady-state' situations, as Banfield terms the habitual and non-controversial, nothing 'happens'. It can, however, be precisely such 'steady-state' situations that provide the key to understanding the nature of a society. It is in these areas of regular political behaviour that the accepted values of the society most strikingly display themselves. Influence habitually wielded without arousing controversy is one of the patterns of the behaviour which distinguishes one society sharply from another.

An example of such a 'steady-state' situation in a democratic society might be the normal and non-controversial processes of holding elections or of making appointments on public bodies such as advisory committees or investigatory commissions. The ordinary workings of capitalism in the west or of social control in the Soviet Union are also not matters of widespread controversy but they grant power to some groups in society and not to others. In addition they are supports for the regimes themselves. Lack of dissent cannot be taken as indicative of the absence of influence. Dahl argues that in polyarchies the political values of the leaders tend to be more coherent than those of the citizens at large, but not substantially different. The temptation to regard this as a disproof of the existence of elitism is understandably strong. It could, however, represent the high-point in the success of an ideology which, according to most elitists, occurs when all segments of the society, leaders and 'mass', concur as to their values.[13] When the ideology enters the ordinary vocabulary of the society, the political and social system and those who wield power within it receive support even from casual conversation. As Marx pointed out, the mere use of the word 'commodity' to describe an 'object' is revealing of a form of society and a form of influence. This consensus – one not only amongst the leaders but also between leaders and the vast majority of the society – will again ensure that some logically possible options will not appear on the agenda, such as the rapid introduction of workers' control of industry in the USA.

Is it permissible to describe societies where there is almost complete consensus as elitist? Dahl thinks not, and presses his point to an extreme and somewhat paradoxical conclusion.[14] Unless, he argues, there are articulated differences of preference between members of a society it is impossible to discover whether a ruling elite exists or not, since one will not be able to cite instances of a ruling elite imposing its will over the preferences of the majority or of other groups. This would mean that a totalitarian regime, in many ways the ideal type of elitist rule, where a complete consensus appears to exist as a result of the control of opinion and expression, could not be described as elitist because no difference of preference could be detected. Indeed, such differences would have to appear before the manipulation of public opinion could be demonstrated. In the case of extreme totalitarianism Dahl's argument is misleading in that an apparent consensus is not the only evidence of elitism. The existence of a coordinated group controlling the content and circulation of news for public consumption would show that an elite held the initiative.

The problem of analysing a consensual situation inside a presumed democracy still remains. A researcher might hypothesise that there must exist certain 'real' or 'objective' interests which are being suppressed through the acceptance of the prevailing ideology that is manipulated, consciously or unconsciously, by the ruling group who stand to gain by that ideology. A natural harmony of interests is rare in politics and one might presume that some persons or groups would have an 'objective interest' in differing publicly. Polsby rejects such a step as impermissible.[15] 'Objective' interests are merely 'constructs of the analyst' which enable him to bring the evidence into line with his theories. If a group fails to differ from the views and policies of the bulk of society the researcher can then fall back on 'false consciousness' to suggest that the group's objective interests were concealed from itself by the prevailing and all-pervading ideology of the society.

That this is a danger is surely undeniable, and Polsby does well to warn against it.[16] However his contention means that the entire elitist analysis of ideology is rejected as irrelevant and unempirical. Only claims and differences brought to the attention of the leaders count as issues.[17] But if writers as various as Marx, Mosca and Weber are anywhere near correct, the ideological factor is a major contribution to both holding society together and securing advantages for the powerful. No person starts off with a blank sheet when making a political decision. Habit and custom, the values of the society, must influence though not determine the direction he takes. Consensus cannot be taken at its face value. It cannot be presumed to indicate the absence of a powerful elite, nor to indicate its existence, since agreement may not necessarily be manipulated. Evidence of the control of information in the society would be relevant. But there seems to be no sure guidance for the researcher here, simply a warning that the ideological dimension cannot be ignored without distortion to the results.

It is the ability to decide the agenda for public consideration that gives the leaderships, even in a polyarchy, an added influence over the rest of the society.[18] If it is they who decide what is an issue, what is the status of matters they decide are not issues? Are they to be presumed non-controversial? Polyarchalists appear to be saying that anyone who feels intensively enough and has sufficient enterprise can get a matter placed on the agenda. This presupposes a commitment to the existing procedures and a facility for organising which, as has been suggested, may go beyond what an already frustrated and alienated minority is prepared to attempt. It also presupposes as well as the lack of legal impediments to participation the absence or unimportance of social and economic pressures upon political action that Hunter and Agger discovered could not be presumed in apparently open communities. The men who were sacked or edged out of their positions, who were ostracised or whose burgeoning radicalism was cut short by threats to their careers are witness to some of the disincentives to participation.[19] The fear and even the unjustified expectation of such sanctions is as important as their actual imposition for understanding power relations.

The considerable criticism of the polyarchal hypothesis probably reflects a fear that it may become a new pluralist orthodoxy and could unintentionally stimulate a new complacency about the working of democratic procedures. There has, perhaps, been in the middle 1960s a feeling amongst some students of politics that its conclusions are irrelevant to the explanation of such phenomena as the mass movements aroused by issues like Vietnam and the 'crisis in the cities'.[20] Political studies frequently reflect the concerns of the immediate period in which they are written, and political events can stimulate research in new directions.

THE NATURE OF DECISION-MAKING

Elitists and pluralists have concentrated their attention on 'decision-making' which is the point at which the possession of power is made manifest. A single minority or a number of minorities are conceived of as making the 'big decisions' which will determine the future course of society. Mills in particular writes in this way. He writes of decisions which 'make history', of 'pivotal positions' and 'pivotal moments', 'command posts' and 'key positions'. But what is a 'big decision', at what point is a 'decision' reached, what is meant by a decision-maker and how is he to be recognised? These are notoriously difficult questions to answer. Here one can only isolate some of the problems.

A 'decision' can always be broken down into a number of stages.[21] There is the stage in which a project is initiated, it is then discussed and perhaps put into a more appealing or consistent shape. There is the stage at which support for the project is mobilised whether by public actions or by private bargaining and exhortation. In the studies by Hunter and Presthus many of the participants and observers believed that the stages of deliberation and mobilisation of support were the crucial 'take-off' points for a policy since 'who' was prepared to give backing was crucial to the policy's success. The next stage is what Agger and his colleagues term 'authoritative consideration' i.e. the consideration of policy alternatives by constitutionally authorised persons. These might in some circumstances be the electorate, in others appointed officials, in others elected rulers. When a policy has been selected this is taken as a decisional outcome. It is promulgated and then put into effect. These several stages are not necessarily chronological in order. In particular, policy deliberation and the organisation of political support frequently overlap and can continue alongside the process of authoritative consideration.

This account of decision-making is more subtle than anything the elitists offered but it is still not complex enough. Firstly, as the authors recognise, a policy may be vetoed before it reaches the stage of authoritative consideration.[22] A decisional veto has been taken somewhere at the stage of policy deliberation or because of crucial resistance when support was being mobilised. Secondly, the process of authoritative consideration can be long and complex, and can be further dissolved into a number of steps, some of which can seem very much like 'decisions'. Thirdly, the formula still offers no rule by which one can recognise a 'decisional outcome'.

Agger's approach may perhaps be filled out by one proposed by W. J. M. Mackenzie.[23] The 'decision' is understood as the formal act which ends the authoritative consideration of the issue. It is, to adapt Hobbes, "the act of will that ends deliberation". A decision defined in this way is procedural in two ways. Firstly, the decision is what J. L. Austin termed a 'performative utterance', meaning a verbal formula such as 'I promise' or 'I decide', which does not describe an act of promising or deciding but is itself the act of promising and deciding, providing that certain necessary social preconditions are fulfilled.[24] These preconditions range from the trivial, such as that all parties understand that the sounds 'I decide' constitute deciding, to the important and complex, such as that the person uttering the words has the authority to say 'I decide' in the circumstances in question. Secondly, Mackenzie suggests that in the case of decisions the necessary preconditions can be explained by H. L. A. Hart's concept of 'the rule of recognition'.[25] Such a rule, written or unwritten, lays down criteria by which anyone can identify who in a community or organisation has the authority to make such performative utterances as 'I decide'.

This formal decision will, in all probability, be taken by a small minority but elitism is not thereby proved. It still seems sensible to go behind the board of directors or the Cabinet minister and wonder whether the 'real decision' had not already been taken. Mackenzie's convincing solution is to insist that the formal performative utterance be regarded as the 'decision' and then to trace the policy and its rivals through the stages of deliberation and mobilisation of support. In the process the policy, usually modified, picks up more and more support from persons and groups with apparent weight in the organisation until a point is reached when the agreement of all that matter has been gained. The outcome is then almost 100 per cent certain, and all that remains to come is the formality of 'the decision'. At earlier stages the outcome was less certain though it is doubtful whether any exact measurement can be made of the likelihood of the decision going one way or the other. Other patterns are possible, however. In particular it may be advisable to seek a 'decision' at an early stage. This will keep the policy moving and the decision will also serve to mobilise opinion in its support.

In routine cases for which there is ample precedent the likely outcome will probably be known earlier; for more unusual cases knowledge of the outcome will probably be delayed. But not even this can be taken as a general rule. Where a policy is required very speedily the essential step may be taken very early and by someone lower in the hierarchy. The formal decision by the minority is then merely a necessary *imprimatur*, and sometimes one that has to be rationalised and defended by the minority if the policy is challenged.

Even adopting this procedure it will not be easy to discover empirically at what point and why the policy is transformed from being a possible to a probable winner. The elitists see decisions as conscious, purposive steps on the analogy of Caesar crossing the Rubicon but, apart perhaps from the formal 'decision' itself, the process towards a collective decision is far less tidy than that. Such an important measure as the 1944 Education Act in Britain might be regarded as a major decision of the sort that an elite would make, but in turn its provisions can be seen as an aggregation of many much smaller agreements and commitments entered into lower down the hierarchy and involving a wider circle of people. The decisional outcome thus reflects an accumulation of steps often involving a host of modifications to the original policy-concessions, additions, syntheses with rival policies. Moreover, some steps often appear crucial to the final outcome only in retrospect whereas at the time they may not have seemed irretrievable moves. The Rubicon may be crossed inadvertently.

Agger and his associates discovered that, despite Dahl's claims concerning the essentially compromising and non-ideological character of democratic decision-making, the communities they studied experienced ideological disputes which resulted in the clear victory of one ideology over another. This certainly has important repercussions for the understanding of American politics in particular. But as a general rule one must beware of treating a 'decision' as an ideological victory for reasons similar to those already given. A piece of legislation is not the implementation of an ideology but the passage of a complex set of regulations which will work in practice. The passage of an act of nationalisation may seem a victory for a socialist ideology and a defeat for the ideology of free enterprise. The drafting and implementation of such legislation will, however, require the assistance of the very interests who were unsuccessful in opposing it. Both sides require the new act to have some degree of success and at this stage the defeated interests can obtain many detailed advantages. The ideological elite thus takes the 'decisions' but the defeated groups still exercise a major influence. Nor can 'decision-makers' start with 'the blank-sheet of infinite possibility'[26] as Mills seems to imagine his pivotal leaders can, being able to smash one structure of institutions and establish a new one, and to transform their own social roles as well as those of others. Decisions are not made in a historical vacuum, and the options facing even a powerful minority are never entirely of its own choosing. The available policies and the resources to hand to put them through will be conditioned by the activities of earlier minorities. Finally, without accepting Polsby's scepticism as to whether any policy outcome reveals the intentions of the policy-makers,[27] it is true to say that elitists tend to ignore the frequency with which decisions have totally unintended consequences. The power to make decisions can still fall short of the power to change or 'make' history.

'BOUNDARY' PROBLEMS

Elitists assume the existence of a 'system' within which the elite exercises supremacy. The system may be an organisation such as a political party, a local community or the nation itself. The dispute between elitists and pluralists has in large part centred on the questions as to whether there is an overlap of personnel between the political, economic and social 'sub-systems' within the overall system, and which sub-system has the greatest influence. This necessarily raises problems as to where the boundaries are between one system or sub-system and another. Some writers, of whom Dahl is one, regard boundary issues as relatively unimportant, being capable of being resolved definitionally.[28] Boundaries must, they suggest, be to some extent arbitrary. Scholars in other disciplines apparently face similar difficulties without agonising over much about the consequences. The historian, for instance, must place some limit in time to the sequence of actions he is studying. The social sciences, however, face a more acute problem in that it often appears as if the boundaries set to an investigation can affect both the outcome of the study and the whole perspective of the research. Agger and his associates note the relevance of political boundaries to estimating influence in the local community, but do not go more deeply into the problem. Amongst the well-known students of community power, Banfield and Presthus are notable for the significance they attach to boundary issues in assessing the structure of influence.[29]

Many decisions which affect a community deeply are not taken politically but are the result of economic activity. The level of wages or investment in the community, for example, have a major impact on its politics. To prove that the politicians are dominant in deciding public issues may be of less importance if these public issues are, as a Marxist would have it, a mere reflection of economic movements. The boundary between the political and the economic can then seem artificial. There is a strong probability that the boundaries of any 'system' of political decision will not coincide with the boundaries of the economic system. Few communities even at national level are self-sufficient enough not to be influenced by economic pressures from outside. At the local community level the economy may be dominated by firms based outside the community. The fortunes and policies of such firms may make a greater impact on the lives of their workers and of others in the community than any decisions taken by a purely local elite, even if it combines wealth, power and status. A very similar situation occurs at the national level where, as is notoriously true of the United Kingdom, international economic pressures can subvert the policies of a national elite. Outside forces narrow the options. National leaders attempting to keep afloat seem a long way from being an elite with the power to 'make history'.

To take the political boundaries of a community as coincident with its 'power boundaries' can also affect any conclusions about the power structure. Any meaningful estimate of the power of a society's leaders must take into account the extent to which they are dependent on decisions by higher authorities. Presthus discovered this to be a major factor differentiating his two communities. 'Riverview' relied much more heavily than 'Edgewood' on state and federal 'largesse' in its major projects. This had the effect of increasing the influence of the politicians and reducing that of other leaders and organised groups, since only the political leaders had access to the influentials in the state capital and in Washington DC. At the same time the freedom of movement of the political leaders was restricted by the extent of the support they obtained from outside; its withdrawal might have seriously affected their influence. Two of 'Riverview's' major decisions – on hospital and school building – were initiated only after the state had put on very severe pressure. Banfield's Chicago study traces the influence of the Illinois Governor and legislature on some of Chicago's decisions and thereby illustrates that the boundary problem does not affect only small communities. That a researcher should be forced to look at the regional, national or even international influences on community power structure is a proper reflection of the practical difficulty of governing any community, large or small, as an autonomous system not needing to resort to outside assistance.[30]

At times it seems that as the boundaries are extended each elite assumes less significance until the very existence of an elite appears to be entirely the product of the research framework. But, as always, such a general rule rapidly meets a counter-example. Where a national elite is extremely remote, physically as in a large state or as a result of poor communication, its policies may have less influence than the local leaders in close contact with the situation; it is a problem common to large states such as China, to big businesses and to many trades unions. The condition of a system's boundaries is a guide to its autonomy and to the autonomy of its elite. In law one way of gauging the independence of a society is to see whether the boundaries of its legal system are intact. If ultimate authority for some of its laws lies in the laws of another society, as in the case of a colony under the ultimate legal control of the mother country, then one can conclude that it is not autonomous. Similarly with any political, economic or social system or sub-system if its influence cannot be explained without widening the boundaries to include other systems then this indicates that the system and its elite lack autonomy. They are not entirely self-moved.

THE 'COSTS' OF INFLUENCE

One of the most damaging criticisms of elitist theorists is that they assume power to be cumulative, that it can be used in a number of issue areas and that the expenditure of influence in one area involves no loss of influence in another. This, however, could be true only in a society in which there was no opposition whatsoever, a pure elitist system which operated without any friction. Even the elitists clearly found it difficult to imagine this as an empirical possibility and wrote instead of the elite inevitably overcoming resistance. Once it is admitted that there exists a number of forces in society with at least some power of resistance then it is necessary to examine the costs incurred by the elite in defeating them.[31] The power of an elite must be measured in terms of the costs of exercising influence. These costs can range from the consumption of effort and time in exercising influence to the cost of the opposition aroused in a group or groups by the expenditure of influence on another group. An 'economy of influence' can be supposed in which each political actor has a limited stock of resources available which he will have to 'spend' in order to gain the maximum return in influence. Policies which already have latent support from most members of the society will need little expenditure of resources. Policies which meet with a great deal of resistance will involve the expenditure of time and effort in mobilising support and persuading the opposition. Such policies may also be very costly if the 'price' of support for them is the grant of concessions in this or some other issue area. Some projects are simply not worth such a price.

Sometimes such costs are methodologically difficult to detect. A project which seems not worth the costs involved may be withdrawn before it becomes public. This is a case of influence being exercised by one group on another without any evidence being available to the analyst. Again the analyst may make presumptions about the objective interests of the parties which can involve him in some highly-questionable counter-factual conditionals: "if the group had followed policy X (which seems *prima facie* to be in its objective interests) it would have met opposition (since it is against the objective interests of other groups) and would have

incurred the considerable costs Y; it therefore did not proceed with policy X".
Even if such an assessment were correct there may be no empirical evidence of
any intention to pursue X.

This is an example of the 'rule of anticipated reactions'[32] according to which
a group may tacitly modify its policy in anticipation of the reactions of other
groups. The rule cuts both ways in that the alleged elite may tacitly make concessions to the other groups or these may not put forward some of their interests as
claims to be considered because they anticipate their automatic rejection by an
elite possessing veto power. This raises a further problem in assessing the significance of consensual situations since they could arise from elite influence, caus-
ing anticipatory withdrawal by the 'mass', or 'mass' influence resulting in anticipatory retractions by the elite. To obtain a full explanation it is thus necessary to
have evidence both of the original policy intentions and the process of revising or
retracting the policy.

To what extent, however, can an elite go on making concessions and still lay
claim to the title of elite? Banfield points out that complete control of a situation
may sometimes be bought but only at a very high price indeed, measured either
by the watering-down of the policy until it gains acceptance, or by the virtual
abandonment of other projects. But again things can be shown to cut both ways.
It could be that frequent use of power may 'diminish' a political actor's resources
for future occasions. Alternatively, frequent exercise of power may *increase* the
stock of resources since others come to expect the actor to take decisions, the
habitual wielding of influence thus becoming regarded as authoritative.

Most of the 'classical elitists' are forced to acknowledge the need for concessions, particularly when it is a matter of the elite's survival. They do not appear,
however, to recognise the implications for the analysis of the elite's situation.
Concessions are not seen as costs which reduce the elite's resources for influence,
but as instances of the skill and flexibility of the elite by which it retains its 'controlling' position. Mosca's account of 'social forces' is a clear instance. Mosca's
ruling class, it will be remembered, maintains itself by adjusting its policies to
meet the claims of the new social forces which constantly arise in a society, and
by incorporating personnel from such social forces into at least the lower stratum
of the ruling class. By this means the ruling class undergoes 'molecular transformation' but still remains a ruling class, having continuity with its predecessors. It
is, however, a far cry from the conception of an elite as a veto group beyond the
control of the other members of the society. Instead, it is close to one version of
what is sometimes termed 'pluralistic elitism' or 'democratic elitism' in which a
coalition of leadership groups represent the chief interest groups in the society.
Mosca, the elitist, often appears as a precursor of pluralism.[33]

There can, as a result, be 'strong' and 'weak' interpretations of elitist theories,
which is one reason why these theories can be so difficult to test. At the one
extreme elitism can imply the ultimate control of all stages of the decisional
process in the whole range of issue areas – initiation, deliberation and authoritative consideration. It can also mean that the elite exercises control by making entry

into it open to the representatives of the major interest groups. This shades off into the much weaker thesis of elite consensus in which several elites are bound together by shared beliefs on procedural and substantive matters. At its most banal it can mean merely the truism that in organised life fewer men issue commands than obey them. When it refers only to the inequalities of resources which certainly exist in any society it ceases to be an elitist doctrine since such inequalities are consistent with forms of democracy as well as with an elite structure.

The student must needs be clear what form of the thesis he is testing, and be on the watch for any tendency on the elitist's part to shift ground from one level of the thesis to another. The guidelines are perhaps still Meisel's three Cs[34] – the degree to which the elite is cohesive, conscious and conspiratorial.

CONCLUDING INJUNCTIONS

This chapter and its predecessor have concentrated on the problems of both elitist and pluralist theses. They have also made so much of the difficulties of empirically deciding between the rival theories that the outlook for research may be in danger of seeming more bleak than it need be. Some comfort may be taken from W. J. M. Mackenzie commenting on this same problem:

> There is a very large body of interesting knowledge, and it is all the more valuable because it serves to sharpen our wits in hair-splitting over concepts and methods. One learns much about American politics by reading either *Who Governs?* or *Community Power Structure*; and if one reads both one learns more than twice as much.[35]

It may seem presumptuous to end this section by offering some injunctions for research, but it is also perhaps advisable to end it with something more substantial than hair-splitting.

The decisional, reputational and institutional approaches have been refined considerably with experience and as a result of criticism. But it is clear that the days of the uni-dimensional approach are over. *Community Power Structure* and *Who Governs?* will remain as seminal works in the field; in particular *Who Governs?* despite all criticism, must survive as an acknowledged masterpiece of political science. For the future, however, research into elites at the community or any other level is likely to attempt, as Presthus has done so well, to integrate the various methods, regarding them as complementary to one another. The work of analysts such as Agger and Presthus may well indicate that elite studies have reached a new stage in which the methods and accumulated knowledge from the period of grand theory and the period of the first empirical studies will be synthesised. Eclecticism can be a virtue in such matters.

Much of the recent work on elites has profited from being comparative. Expense tends to make this difficult at the national level, though the comparison of specialist elites is likely to be encompassed more easily. Well-financed surveys such as that into 'civic culture' led by Almond and Verba have turned up some information but tend not to possess the depth found in a community study. Community studies are therefore likely to deal, as do Presthus and Agger, with two or more societies which may be expected in advance to differ in relevant respects.

The works of Presthus and Agger set two further trends which ought to be followed. Firstly, the system must be studied over time. Time is a central element in any political actor's calculations. Elitists have seemingly been reluctant to lay down any time span which could help test their laws – how soon will an elite meet its inevitable downfall and be replaced by another? Is a leadership with its eye constantly on the electoral clock to be termed as an elite of power? Will a decisional victory still seem so when its outcome can be measured in detail a year or so on? The 'victory' may not even appear to have been a point of decision when the decisional process is looked at in retrospect. All the communities in *The Rulers and the Ruled* were examined over time involving revisiting the communities to examine the course of events after the major research period. Banfield, using his cost/benefit analysis, had also shown that both costs and benefits are calculated over time.

Secondly, leadership must be examined in relation to the mass. This means not merely the comparison of their social backgrounds with those of the society in general but the study of ideology, of the values held by both leaders and led, of the significance of the habitual exercise of influence and of the extent of alienation the various groups feel from the political system. It involves the awkward task of examining who loses and who does not even participate, and why interests do not necessarily get translated into claims. In the end it involves deciding whether man is, as Dahl would have it, simply not a political animal[36] or whether, as some of his critics would have it, the apathy characteristic of so many citizens in modern democracy is the *effect* of the political system which the critics feel is implicitly defended by Dahl.[37] This theme of man as political animal, as participant or member of the mass, has in fact been central to all the normative discussions of the significance of elites for democracy. It is to these discussions that the final chapter turns.

NOTES

1   Dahl, *Modern Political Analysis*, Ch. 5.
2   The *Sociological Imagination*, Oxford University Press, New York, 1959. References to Evergreen edition, New York, 1961, p. 204.
3   *Community Power and Political Theory*, pp. 100–4.
4   *The Sociological Review*, Vol. III, 1955, pp. 279–94 and Vol. IV, 1956, pp. 5–30.
5   See the discussion above, pp. 100–2, of Presthus.

6 See below, p. 119, on the 'rule of anticipated reactions'.

7 *Capitalism, Socialism and Democracy*, Allen and Unwin, London. 4th edition, 1954.

8 *Community Power and Political Theory*, p. 118.

9 Polsby, *Community Power and Political Theory*, pp. 118-20.

10 See Ch. 6.

11 Hunter, *Community Power Structure*, pp. 218–9; Agger, *et al.*, *The Rulers and the Ruled*, p. 307.

12 *Political Influence*, Free Press, New York, 96, pp. 9–10.

13 See Ch. 2 above.

14 See his penetrating article, 'A Critique of the Ruling Elite Model', *American Political Science Review*, Vol. LII, 1958, pp. 463–9.

15 *Community Power and Political Theory*, p. 23.

16 See below for further discussion on this point.

17 Dahl, *Who Governs?* p. 92.

18 See P. Bachrach and M. Baratz, 'Two Faces of Power', *American Political Science Review*, Vol. LVI, Dec. 1962, pp. 947–52.

19 Hunter, *Community Power Structure*, Ch. 7; Agger *et al. The Rulers and the Ruled*, pp. 85–7, 480–97.

20 But see Dahl, 'The City in the Future of Democracy', *American Political Science Review*, LXI, 4, Dec. 1967, pp. 953–70.

21 The following analysis is derived from Agger, Goldrich and Swanson, *The Rulers and the Ruled*, pp. 40–51.

22 See Bachrach and Baratz, 'Two Faces of Power', *American Political Science Review*, Dec. 1962.

23 *In Politics and Social Science*, Penguin, Harmondsworth, 1967, pp. 232–4, 279–80, and 'Models of Collective Decision-Making', *Social Sciences: Problems and Orientations*, Mouton for UNESCO, The Hague, May 1968, pp. 356–70.

24 See J. L. Austin, 'Performative Utterances', *Philosophical Papers*, Oxford University Press, London 1961, pp. 220–39; *How to do things with Words*, Oxford University Press, London, 1962. Austin's discussion of non-verbal acts may be ignored for purposes of this discussion.

25 *The Concept of Law*, Oxford University Press, London, 1961, Chs. V and VI.

26 M. Oakeshott, 'Political Education', *Rationalism in Politics*, Methuen, London, 1962, p. 112.

27 *Community Power and Political Theory*, p. 91.

28 *Modern Political Analysis*, p. 24.

29 See also A. J. Vidich and J. Bensman, *Small Town in Mass Society*, Princeton University Press, Princeton, 1958.

30 Dahl has a rather different case of the impact of political boundaries. The fact that most economic notables lived outside the New Haven boundaries disqualified them from participating in decisions affecting the school system.

31 There has been a considerable amount of work on cost/benefit analysis. E. C. Banfield's *Political Influence* is an excellent example of its application to problems of political influence. J. M. Buchanan and G. Tullock, *The Calculus of Consent*, Michigan University Press, Ann Arbor, 1962, and A. Downs, *An Economic Theory of Democracy*, Harper and Row, New York, 1957, are noted theoretical expositions. See also B. Barry, *Political Argument*,

Routledge, London, 1965, esp. pp. 242–85. Introductory treatment will be found in W. J. M. Mackenzie, *Politics and Social Science*, pp. 144–52, 236–9. For its use in classical political theory see S. Wolin on 'Machiavelli and the Economy of Violence' in *Politics and Vision*, Allen and Unwin, London, 1961.

32 C. J. Friedrich, *Man and his Government*, McGraw-Hill, New York, 1963, Ch.11.
33 See the following chapter.
34 See above, Ch. 2.
35 *Politics and Social Science*, p. 235.
36 *Modern Political Analysis*, Ch. 6.
37 See J. Walker, 'A Critique of the Elitist Theory of Democracy', *American Political Science Review*, Vol. LX, No. 2, 1966, pp. 285–95 and Dahl's reply in the same number. Also P. Bachrach, *The Theory of Democratic Elitism*, Little, Brown, Boston and Toronto, 1967.

chapter six | elites and democratic theory

Is the existence of elites compatible with the existence of democracy? Classical elitists such as Mosca and Pareto declared that a prime aim of their work was to demolish the myths of democracy. They set out to show that the notion that the people or a majority of the people ruled was a chimera, and that, whatever the form of government, the effective rulers constituted a narrow elite. Majoritarian democracy in any strict sense of the term was, in their view an impossibility, confirmed by the experience of history. However, the rival pluralist theory that society was composed of a number of groups, each with its inner group of leaders, argued that democracy was consistent with the existence of a multiplicity of elites.

Such a dispute is not capable of a ready solution. It is not possible to answer such questions by empirical research without first clarifying one's terms. The degree of consciousness, cohesion and conspiracy within and amongst the elites is, in principle, capable of being discovered empirically despite the considerable methodological problems that have been raised in preceding chapters. The definition of democracy is another matter, and one which has aroused considerable controversy in the context of elite theorising.

The attempts to square the existence of elites with the existence of democracy has led to a dispute about some of the fundamental issues of politics. 'Democracy' and 'democratic' have become in the twentieth century words which imply approval of the society or institution so described. This has necessarily meant that the words have become debased in that they have almost ceased without further definition to be of any use in distinguishing one particular form of government from another. They are words which few political protagonists are prepared to concede to their rivals for their exclusive property. Political scientists moreover are not ready to see these words appropriated to describe political systems which do not measure up to what they expect of a democracy.

It might be said that the disputes among the writers cited in this book are merely about words and that it does not matter in the least how a word is defined for matters of analysis, provided the definition is stated and used consistently. Many students of the social sciences are understandably reluctant to accept this. It is undeniable that words change in meaning and that a term like 'democracy' cannot be restricted entirely to its original usage. Nevertheless, when a word is used in a novel fashion the innovator usually wishes to indicate that the new use is one which is intimated in the old, that it is a mere extension of familiar usage. There can come a point, as there has in the discussion of the relation between elites and democracy, when some people attempt to call a halt to such extensions and assert that the meaning has been stretched so far that it bears no relation to the established usage. They argue that it is now used to describe a condition of affairs different in kind as well as in degree from that for which it had previously been used. It is claimed that the new use is misleading and should be abandoned or else be qualified adjectivally as in 'direct' democracy, 'guided' democracy or 'liberal' democracy.

Controversy has surrounded all attempts to stretch the meaning of democracy to accommodate the findings of elitists and elite pluralists. Critics of such efforts claim that they involve a major redefinition of democracy which loses sight of its original meaning of the power of (hence rule by) the people. Instead it is used to describe a situation in which only a very small proportion of the population is directly involved in ruling or making significant decisions. This raises important issues for democratic thought. To what extent is a high degree of political participation necessary for a political system to warrant the title 'democracy' or for it to survive as a democracy? In a form of democracy where elites are regarded by government and by citizens as the legitimate influentials what political activities is the individual expected to perform? Is he merely a voter or one who transmits his claims to the leaders of his group for them to act upon? Alternatively, is it basic to the conception of democracy that each member of the society is expected to be an active citizen and that he ought to recognise his responsibility to cultivate a civil spirit and participate fully in the society's affairs?

Ultimately the debate has concerned the nature of 'the political' itself. It has been asked whether the boundaries of political activity might not be widened so that other areas of human activity might be imbued with political significance. Economic life in particular might be 'politicised' by subordinating industrial corporations and businesses to some form of popular control by elected workers' councils or an elected body of shareholders, consumers, employees. The object would be to democratise the work situation, encourage participation and limit elite control. Against this it is argued that such direct participation is unnecessary and that with a much more limited conception of the role of politics it is still perfectly possible to satisfy the basic demands of a society in a democratic fashion.

The debate about democratic principles has not been conducted simply in terms of abstract theory. It has already been shown that there have been disputes amongst empirical political scientists and sociologists as to the tendencies of various research techniques to discover one form of political structure rather than another and that this has led to wide differences over the interpretations of the results of the enquiries. Moreover some empirical studies have been accused of having a fundamental bias owing not only to the methodology but to the political preferences of their authors. Terms such as 'pluralism' or 'democratic elitism', which would be more appropriate as labels for ideologies, have been applied to pieces of empirical research. Studies which declare themselves to be objective accounts of the way in which a political system actually works have been criticised as being conscious or unconscious defences of the system and as being vitiated by their acceptance of an inadequate definition of democracy.

'PLURALISM' OR 'DEMOCRATIC ELITISM'?

The view that a multiplicity of elites or leadership groups is compatible with democracy has been termed 'pluralist' by its exponents, whether empirical researchers such as Polsby and Dahl or political philosophers such as William Kornhauser.[1] Its opponents have coined the terms 'democratic elitism' or 'the elite theory of democracy' to describe the same view.[2] Mosca, the classical elitist, was amongst the first to offer a mode of reconciling elites with democracy. In his later years he came to see the virtues of the nineteenth century liberal political system which he had exposed and ridiculed when younger. The closing chapters of *The Ruling Class* reflect this changing attitude. Society is seen as composed of many social forces and interests, whose leading personnel have to be assimilated by the ruling class if the latter is to survive. Mosca acknowledged even in his earlier years that liberal democracy offered a greater opportunity than other forms of government for the social forces to make their interests felt, and this belief appears to have become firmer in his later work. Nevertheless, Mosca never permits his pluralist moments to totally outweigh his basic monism. However important the plurality of social forces may be, there is still in Mosca's view a single ruling class into which the leaders of the forces must be assimilated if they are to be influential.

Joseph A. Schumpeter's *Capitalism, Socialism and Democracy*,[3] which first appeared in 1942, made a major impact on democratic theorising. It has been regarded[4] as the chief contribution to redefining democracy so as to accommodate an elitist situation. Schumpeter's now celebrated definition of democracy is "that institutional arrangement for arriving at political decisions in which individuals acquire the power to decide by means of a competitive struggle for the people's vote".[5] One appeal of this definition is its apparent 'realism'. It seems to fit the kinds of political systems characterised by political parties competing for election which are termed democracies in ordinary speech. It avoids any connotation of direct democracy in which the people rule directly – a conception seemingly too 'idealistic' or outmoded for twentieth-century use. The definition recognises, as Schumpeter pointed out, the vital role played by leadership in modern 'democracies', earlier theories having "attributed to the electorate an altogether unrealistic degree of initiative". Ruling could be in the hands only of the leadership group which was successful in the electoral competition.

One of Schumpeter's most crucial steps, as Bachrach has pointed out, is that he defines democracy as a *method* which is well designed to produce a strong, authoritative government. No ideals are attached to the definition of democracy itself. It does not in itself imply any notions of civic responsibility or of widespread political participation, or any idea of the ends of man. Indeed, as Schumpeter recognises, pursuing the democratic method may result in an elected government which democratically denies men rights which might seem fundamental. Liberty and equality which have been part and parcel of past definitions of democracy are regarded by Schumpeter as not being integral parts of such a definition, however worthy they may be as ideals.

The chief part played by the citizen of Schumpeter's democracy is the acceptance or rejection of the political leaders. Schumpeter is prepared to describe democracy as 'the rule of the politician' and indeed a major implication of his argument is that the political leadership, once elected, should be permitted to get on with the job of governing with little interference from the citizens. The voters must "respect the division of labour between themselves and the politicians they elect".[6] The citizen has the right, of course, to participate through membership and support of a political party, or even to attempt to cut a path of his own independently of party. Nevertheless, actions such as putting pressure on MPs through constant petitioning, or a bombardment of letter writing, which might impede the politicians' freedom to govern ignore the division of labour and might, in Schumpeter's view, be discouraged or even banned altogether.

Schumpeter's conception of the political leader is almost akin to that of Max Weber. He is the person granted the authority to decide, and must be allowed the freedom necessary if he is to deliberate and act in a responsible manner. This does not mean, however, that the political leadership wields absolute power. It is restricted by the competitive nature of democracy. It must draw up policies to gain more support from the electorate than its opponents can obtain. In this, too, the leaders hold the initiative, and the people respond.[7] The leaders trade in votes and the better the combination of policies they sell the more votes they can obtain through appealing to a wider section of the political market. Dahl's description of polyarchy is couched in similar terms. Even when discussing the element of competition in democracy Schumpeter stresses the competition between the members of the political elite itself. The chief danger to the existing leadership comes from other ambitious politicians looking for a pretext to stake a claim for the foremost position rather than from any movement amongst the electorate itself. Such a movement is only effective when harnessed by one of the leaders to his own or his party's ends.

Schumpeter's discussion pays scarcely any attention to 'intermediary' groups which operate between the political leadership and the individual citizens. He does not mention the 'group theories' of the political process. More recent theorists of democracy have built up on Schumpeter's analysis by taking into account these organised groups – churches, trades unions, business associations, consumer groups, etc. According to these theories each group represents the interests of its members and attempts to put pressure on the political leadership in order to secure the acceptance of its policies. Each group is in competition with other groups and, in the conditions of scarcity with which politics deals, not all interests are capable of being satisfied. Nevertheless, it is often claimed that all claims are listened to.[8] The ultimate authority to decide between the claims lies with the political leadership, but many claims, on this theory, are settled below the level of the political arena. Each group sorts out the claims which it believes worth putting forward for political consideration. Others it can satisfy internally or can persuade its members to abandon. Still others it can settle by negotiation and compromise with the other groups without the wider public being involved through its political representatives. Many of the activities of the unions and business associations can be settled in this way.

As was mentioned in Chapter Three, such intermediary groups are normally headed by a small leadership group. It is these leaders who filter the claims of their members so that only those which are most significant or which offer the greatest promise of success go forward for public consideration. It is these elites (in general an appropriate term since they act as a group and normally are able to control their followers and the access to the leading positions) which effect the compromises between the groups. Although the theory states that these elites are competitive and largely self-cancelling, the criticism that the very contacts between the elites can just as readily lead to a consensus amongst them appears *prima facie* equally valid, as has been indicated in the discussion in Chapter Three.

Empirical studies such as those by Dahl, Banfield or Presthus, take the existence of such intermediary groups for granted and are, ostensibly at least, only concerned to explain the part they play in the politics of the communities studied. Other recent writers have offered a theoretical defence of the groups and their leaderships, claiming that both are essential to the working of democracy and to safeguarding liberty. The most notable of such defences are those by Giovanni Sartori in his *Democratic Theory*, published in 1962, and William Kornhauser's *The Politics of Mass Society*, which appeared in 1960. Earlier Raymond Aron had argued along similar lines in an important article on 'Social Structure and the Ruling Class'.[9]

It is Kornhauser's contention that the intermediary groups in pluralist liberal democracy safeguard it from the dangers of either totalitarianism on the one hand or 'mass society' on the other. Where intermediate relations are unavailable individuals are left, according to Kornhauser, in an atomised condition lacking the information, the contacts and the cohesion to take political initiatives. In this atomised state they may become apathetic towards politics. It is an apathy, however, which conceals fundamental discontent which can be manipulated and mobilised by national elites. In Kornhauser's terms people in a mass are readily 'available' for mobilisation by an elite. The mass may be led in directions which result in the overthrow of the existing regime and its replacement by the new elite. Where this elite has totalitarian intentions mass society, which is free even if apathetic, is replaced by elite control of all social activities. Participation is encouraged in new intermediate groups which are not, however, autonomous as in pluralist society but are elite controlled.

The autonomous intermediate groups of pluralist democracy provide, in

Kornhauser's view, the means for real participation. They constitute the framework in which the individual can develop his interest in and contribute towards matters which concern him, from civic affairs to the education of his children.[10] They can also satisfy many of his claims at the intermediate level. In this way they protect the national elites from direct pressure from the people. Such pressure Kornhauser regards as dangerous since it tends in his view to be ill informed and extremist when not restrained by the values and moderating, comprising experience of the intermediary groups. Where there is direct and ready access to the national elite there is in consequence a concentration of national organisations facing a very individualistic society – a classic elitist and also potentially a totalitarian situation. For these reasons the groups should have the maximum self-government possible. Close ties such as are provided by the family are no substitute, according to this argument, for the political education provided by intermediary groups.

The competition between the elitists of these groups is on this view the bulwark of liberty, as is the fact (assumed by such democratic theories[11]) that individuals will belong to more than one group at any time. These multiple affiliations will prevent any tendency by one group to absorb or destroy all other groups. As in Schumpeter the elites, both at national and intermediary level, should be allowed considerable freedom of action, and once granted authority the division of labour between elite and non-elite should be preserved. The non-elite should have considerable opportunity to select the elites, but its participation is largely limited to election-times.

Sartori's view of democracy is in all essentials similar to that of Schumpeter and Kornhauser. Like Schumpeter he regards democracy as a procedure in which leaders compete at elections for authority to govern. Like Kornhauser he argues that democrats should recognise the essential role of leadership without feeling any sense of guilt.[12] Elites are not an imperfection in a democracy but, where they are themselves democratic, are the guarantor of the system. Democracy is, for Sartori, as much dependent on the quality of its leaders as any other regime. He regards it as anachronistic to be defending democracy against an aristocratic ruling class when the real danger is the absence of leadership which could result in the mass being exploited by antidemocratic counter-elites.[13]

For Sartori a prime element of democracy is that it is a procedure to bolster the authority of the political leadership. Any notion of a self-governing people is a delusion, part of the out-moded myths of democratic theory – a sentiment shared by such elitists as Mosca and Pareto. In Sartori's democracy the people assume a governmental role only at elections. The object of elections, moreover, is not to promote popular participation but to select leaders. The best form of election will be that which selects the best qualified leaders, and Sartori instances J. S. Mill's scheme for plural voting by the better educated.[14] That such leaders might group themselves together as elites which consciously attempt to mould public opinion would be, for Sartori, a welcome development.

Supporting his case by the findings of studies of voting behaviour, Sartori argues that the voter is, on average, poorly informed, unperceptive and often unin-terested. His opinions are not his own but moulded by class, group membership and family. Public opinion never originates ideas; it is influenced before itself attempting to influence.[15] There would therefore be good justification for an elite of quality to shape and educate public opinion, especially where the elite is in competition with other elites. Not that public opinion even then will weigh the alternative information and exhortations. A plurality of opinion-leaders will, how-ever, make for a plurality of opinions and force the competing leaderships to meet a greater range of claims than would otherwise be the case.

In all these theories, whether they be called pluralist or elitist, individual par-ticipation in public affairs is not itself an important ideal. The real participants are the members of the political elites in the parties and in public office, and the elites of the many competing intermediary groups. The defenders of such 'democracies' argue that large-scale participation is undesirable and even that a little apathy con-cerning national affairs does no great harm. Their argument would seem to be sup-ported by the findings of political scientists who have studied voting behaviour particularly in the USA which bears some resemblance to the democratic system which these democrats admire. Participation, repeated studies have found, is low both in quantity and quality. Yet the system survives. The conclusion sometimes drawn from this is that participation is not a necessary feature of democracy and that man is not by nature a political animal.

CLASSICAL DEMOCRACY

The critics of elitist democracy have been quick to point out the fallacy of suppos-ing that empirical evidence concerning contemporary democracies can be taken as a refutation of what they regard as the still viable ideals of 'classical democracy'. Graeme Duncan and Steven Lukes offer one of the shrewdest and most succinct criticisms of the 'category mistake' involved in refuting the older theories of democracy by reference to empirical realities.[16] Democratic theorists such as Rousseau or John Stuart Mill were proposing 'normative' theories which they recognised to be at odds with a reality which they sought to change. Both were aware, Duncan and Lukes point out, of the difficulties of translating their goals into reality. Rousseau's starting point is with "men as they are, and laws as they might be", i.e. with man's potentialities for political action and with laws which, while appropriate to man's capacities, aim at establishing a framework for a freer and more moral society than had existed hitherto.

The failure of contemporary societies to achieve such goals cannot in itself demonstrate that they are inherently incapable of achievement. Empirical study could refute these democratic aims only by showing that they were humanly impossible to achieve. It can also show that to attain the goals would involve a radical change in society which would meet with such great resistance that the idea would properly be called Utopian, or that such a move would have consequences which most people would regard as undesirable. If 'classical democracy' or Rousseau's ideal society does not exist it is not thereby proved that it is impossible. It is always open to the defenders of such views to say that there has never been a real attempt to put 'true democracy' into practice. Men have never, it might be said, stood up for their ideals and made the choices which might translate ideals into reality. Moreover, the ideals would still stand as goals towards which men should move.

It would appear that in response to the gradual assimilation of elite theory into democratic theory there has emerged a growing number of defenders of what they take to be an older and more fruitful conception of democracy. Amongst the most prominent of recent writers who have argued in this way are Henry S. Kariel, in *The Decline of American Pluralism*[17] and *The Promise of Politics*,[18] T. B. Bottomore, in *Elites and Society*,[19] Jack L. Walker, in his article 'A Critique of the Elite Theory of Democracy'[20] and Peter Bachrach, in *The Theory of Democratic Elitism*.[21] The article by Duncan and Lukes, though chiefly methodological, is clearly sympathetic to classical democracy, and the same sentiment may be detected in the opening chapters of Presthus's *Men at the Top* where the contradiction between the older and the new theories of democratic pluralism is detected, and certain inadequacies of the newer theory are pointed out.

The appeal of the 'classical theory' to these writers lies in its emphasis on the importance of widespread political participation on the part of the citizens of a democracy. This emphasis often went to the point of asserting that participation was an obligation on each member of society, a part of his civic duty. In a democratic Greek city-state government by the people had a real meaning. Citizens had an equal right to public office and to membership of the assembly. Inspired partly by this Greek ideal of democracy and partly by the ideals of civic virtue associated with classical republican regimes, such as that of ancient Rome, Rousseau further developed the notion of a participating democracy. Again government by the people was seen as the goal, even if only attainable in a city-state. The assembled sovereign people was to exercise direct legislative authority. For Rousseau the individual citizen found freedom in participating in making the laws of his community and then, in his capacity as a subject, obeying the laws he himself made. The individual demonstrated his capacity as a moral being in and through his participation in the decision-making of his community. This participation was less a right than a duty. In classical Greek terms man was a political animal in that it was through political activity that he realised his own capacities. The ideal constitution must be such as not only to provide opportunities for participation but positively to encourage it. The aim should be to enable the good man to be the good citizen.

In the liberal democratic thought of J. S. Mill the notion of political participation was again central. In common with Rousseau he regarded participation in politics or in any other area of collective activity as an education in the exercise of responsibility by, in fact, exercising it. Participation was consequently an essential part of the process of improving 'character'. Apathy or the lack of opportunity for participation would, in modern society, lead only to irresponsibility. Self-help was the ideal, but Mill warned against assuming that a system of majoritarian elective government was to be identified with individual self-government. The aim should again be to reform political societies so that they fostered the virtue of self-help by broadening the opportunities for participation.

It is this aim which the critics of 'democratic elitism' would like to see followed in modern society. Participation should be re-emphasised as an integral part of the ideal and indeed the definition of democracy. The old definition of 'government by the people' should be given new meaning. Their claim is that the elitist democrats, in empirical writings as well as openly normative works, have corrupted this original meaning and have identified 'democracy' with the procedures and goals of what are nowadays termed democracies. Bachrach, Walker and the others are amongst the first to admit that present-day 'democracies' are very far both from fulfilling the classical ideals and from possessing the institutional arrangements for the political involvement they desire. Their response is that modern 'democracy' has taken a wrong anti-populist turning and the modern theory of democracy has followed suit.

Whether the theory of classical democracy was ever so monistic as its recent defenders appear to claim is, as Dahl himself points out in his reply to Walker,[22] extremely doubtful. Whilst Rousseau's *Social Contract* is profoundly anti-elitist in character, the same is not so unambiguously true of John Stuart Mill. John Stuart Mill,[23] as has been mentioned already, believed that responsible political participation required education and experience. Consequently he recommended extra votes for the better educated and for those in positions requiring responsibility and skills from managers to foremen. Literacy should be a qualification for the vote. The object was to ensure the appearance of 'the very elite of the country' in Parliament. By the standards of argument they would introduce into debate the members of the elite would, Mill believed, raise the level of political argument both in Parliament and in the nation. Only through means such as these, Mill declared, would democracy "have its occasional Pericles, and its habitual group of superior and guiding minds".[24]

Admittedly Mill is not an elitist in the sense that he expects his elite to form a conscious, cohesive and conspiratorial group. It will not form a distinct elite party. Its votes in parliament will not outweigh those of the less educated. It is also true that Mill expected his educational qualifications for entry into the political arena to go alongside the great extension of schooling and of practical education through greater opportunities for participation in other areas of human life, thereby allowing more to enter political life. Nevertheless, Mill's motive was to alleviate the dangers to individual freedom and to the stability of parliamentary government which he foresaw might arise with the extension of political rights to the masses. Such a development would, he thought, bring class legislation by representatives led by a public opinion which was low in intelligence.[25] It might reasonably be asked, therefore, whether Sartori or Kornhauser differ very much in their concern for democratic leadership from Mill, one of the 'great names' of so-called classical democracy.

THE RADICAL ALTERNATIVE

The alternative theory of democracy offered by such writers as Kariel, Bachrach and Bottomore I shall call 'radical democracy', at the risk of describing as a school what is rather a common disposition, and of ignoring the ways in which their views differ. The theory of 'radical democracy' centres on the need to revive a sense of civic spirit throughout society. 'Radical democrats' would reform the institutions and attitudes of twentieth century democracy so that the participation of the ordinary citizen in decision-making would be regarded as normal, legitimate and desirable. They accuse the democratic elitists of having been so concerned with the stability of the political system that they have ignored the ideals which are embedded in democracy. Participation, it is claimed, far from being an ideal is often discouraged by the democratic elitists as possibly subversive of democracy as it now functions. The apathy which empirical social and political science discovers amongst voters and which is used to bolster the normative case for democratic elitism is, the 'radical democrats' suggest, not something which is in the nature of man but is conditioned by society. Man can be a political animal only in a society in which he is encouraged to be political. Evidence of apathy need only be one index of the extent to which a society has fallen short of the democratic ideals, not proof of their impracticality.

The 'radical democrats', despite their admiration for 'classical democracy', do not believe that the city-state democracy of the Greeks, or of Rousseau or the New England town meeting can be revived and displace the modern state. They do, however, regard the ideals implicit in such past politics as still viable. Societies can and ought at least to strive for greater equality of opportunity for people to share in the decision-making which affects their lives. In part this will involve the simple re-emphasising of the older civic virtues of participation. People might be encouraged to make greater use of the facilities they already possess. Attendance at political meetings, voting at elections, local and national, could be encouraged, as could similar use of the rights of trades union members.

Such steps will, however, be futile, the 'radical democrats' suggest, if the structure of society is not reformed so as to make participation more meaningful to the individual. If the citizen will not come to the state, then the state must go to the citizen. And this is so not only of the state but of all the major institutions and organisations of modern society. Bottomore and Bachrach in particular – Kariel appears more cautious when it comes to details – wish for the traditional distinction between the political and the non-political to be broken down. The object is not that of the sociologist who wishes to demonstrate that the political is an epiphenomenon of the social. The aim is rather to politicise the non-political, to show the analogies between what are acknowledged to be political institutions and what received opinion regards as non-political institutions. They suggest that political procedures are appropriate to what has been regarded as the non-political arena.

If national politics may seem remote to the man in the street his work is certainly not. One's occupation and the conditions in which one works are amongst the most influential factors in shaping one's life. In contemporary society decisions affecting work situations are generally taken by industrial managers in greater or lesser consultation with union leaders. Participation is limited. 'Radical democrats' argue that such a situation is ripe for politicisation. The large organisations increasingly characteristic of modern industry are in a position to allocate values for the society but their accountability to the society is obscure. They may have a responsibility to their shareholders, and may be checked intermittently by the government. 'Radical democrats', however, fear that elitist democracy does not provide for sufficient sanctions against such a powerful business elite and that the elitist notion of pluralism, in its insistence on the maximum possible self-government by the elites, will rely for restraint too much on the conscience of the elite.

Not only does such an economic system fall short on accountability, its contact with the public comes more from market surveys than from any direct, voluntary involvement by the people. Manipulation, C. Wright Mills suggests, is then a substitute for authority.[26] To overcome these tendencies both Bottomore and Bachrach advocate the democratisation of industry. There should be an extension not of consultation but of direct participation in the decision-making of industry. Bottomore argues[27] in favour of the introduction of workers' councils to manage public industry. At the same time all large industry should be publicly owned though not state-managed, as most industrialised concerns are at present, since a state-elite is as remote as a private elite from those working in the industry.

Bachrach[28] looks to a wider membership of what he calls the 'corporate constituency'. Employees should be joined by shareholders (public ownership not being essential to Bachrach's argument), suppliers and consumers (who should be backed by research facilities by a government Department of Consumers). Trades unions should not, in Bachrach's opinion, be members of the managerial body. Their duty is to act as an opposition party defending the rights of their members and promoting working conditions. This role would be compromised by managerial involvement. It is not to be assumed that the interests of the worker as producer will inevitably coincide with his interests as a worker, thereby rendering union activity superfluous.

The radical democrats would adopt a similar approach to political institutions. Political authority should be decentralised. (Kariel seems to be an exception, believing that only greater power and participation at the centre can counteract quasi-monopolies in the society and economy.)[29] Local and regional governments, being less remote, facilitate participation and when they are granted real powers they can appear meaningful to the local population. Advocates of greater power at the local and regional levels would counter the evidence of even greater apathy towards such politics than towards national affairs by saying that effective local government had not been attempted in recent times. The local community has in many countries become so heavily dependent on the direction and financing of the national government as to seem meaningless.

In Britain, where there has been a highly centralised political system for some 250 years, pressures have been growing of late for greater devolution of governmental power. This has come not only from the nationalists in Scotland and Wales but from local leaders elsewhere and from political observers who favour regional governmental bodies. Existing local governments would not be adequate, even the larger ones being too small for any real independence from the centre. They would at best form part of a tiered organisation, being the point of closest contact with the citizen. These regional bodies would not be merely advisory councils drawing up plans to be acted upon at the centre but authoritative governing bodies. With a number of such bodies, each with its tiered organisation, the opportunities for individuals to participate directly in government or to influence government would be very considerably increased.

These Rousseauistic tendencies to smaller-scale groupings are often castigated as being not simply Utopian but regressive. It is argued that without large-scale organisation and central control the levels of industrial production and the material standards of living could not be maintained. The classical elitists, particularly Michels, had already held that the imperatives of command ruled out equality of decision-making.[30] Complete equality in making decisions is undoubtedly impossible, but the radical case is that the opportunities for participation can be greatly extended without danger, and that the narrower group of inner decision-makers can be brought under much more effective control. Indeed, equality appears to be less important than liberty, understood as self-development, to Bachrach, Kariel and Walker, though not to Bottomore.

Reactions to the charge of the inefficiency of a participant democracy of this radical kind appear to be of two kinds. One argument, derivable from Marx, is that automation will increase production at the same time as providing the leisure for increased activity in any distinctively human activity, from politics to art. Part of the Marxian argument is also that the sense and fact of participation, of being in control of one's own life, will increase the individual's vigour and result in higher rates of production.[31] A second argument offered by Kariel,[32] and coming more appropriately from a society with a very high standard of living, is that it may be necessary to choose between efficiency and human goals such as liberty or 'self-development'. The notion of costs must, he suggests, be broadened to include costs to the good life for the individual as well as monetary costs.

Another criticism levelled against the lack of realism alleged to be basic to 'radical democracy' is that it fails to take account of the need for expert leadership. Such a view of democracy clearly does place less emphasis on individual leadership and more on consultation and collective action. To this it is objected that the increase in the complexity of government and of the economy requires much greater technical expertise. Without leaders possessing expert knowledge democracy will, it is argued, not be able to compete with other regimes.[33] Such leadership can be recruited in a manner compatible with democracy only by granting each individual equal opportunity to rise in society on the basis of intelligence and effort. So far as is possible every child should start on an equal footing, no privileged education being purchasable. The starting point would be egalitarian in the extreme if really translated into practice, but the outcome would be consciously inegalitarian. It would not necessarily be elitist in that the leadership might be simply a category of meritorious individuals, though it might be expected that the tendency to form a technocratic elite would be strong.

To this meritocratic notion of education and society is usually opposed an idea of education towards a 'common culture'. The object of such education is not so much to produce the exceptional few but to give the whole population a grounding in a basic culture and subsequently to encourage each individual to develop whatever abilities he possesses. Each individual would be encouraged to regard any skill, not merely the academic ones, as of equal value. As Kariel argues,[34] the emphasis in such a theory of education is less on the great works, which he regards as a bonus or fortunate by-product of an activity, than on having people perform the activity themselves. The education should aim at enhancing the effectiveness of individuals. Every educational discipline, for Kariel, can transcend formal schooling and confront the individual with new possible social relations. Education consists, he suggests, of a variety of 'rehearsals for public life'.

DEGREES OF DEMOCRACY?

Democratic elitists show a concern for a range of political values of which the central appear to be liberty, stability and legitimacy, the latter to be achieved by means of the electoral system. Stability is largely achieved through multiple membership of competing intermediary groups whose elites will defend the system against threats arising from either one would-be dominant elite or from the masses. Participation and equality are peripheral values, participation by the non-elite being welcomed by the democratic elitists only in so far as it is necessary for the legitimising process and equality in so far as it does not undermine the protective positions of the elites. The view of man held by the democratic elitist, is one with a long tradition in liberal thought, and is to be found in Hobbes, Hume and Madison. In politics all men are to be presumed to be knaves even if in truth all men are not knaves. Only if the presumption of selfishness and potential hostility is made will the society be ready to deal with the few who do act in that way. The pluralist elite structure is thus ready to counteract the dangers of both totalitarian and mass society. For the most part, societies will, in the democratic elitists' view, be more stable the more their members satisfy themselves within the intermediary groups rather than through politics.

The view of man held by the 'radical democrats' is more generous if not necessarily more correct. Its antecedents can be traced in, amongst others, Rousseau and Marx. Their central concerns are with participation and self-development which they regard as necessary conditions for a humane control of the forces in modern society. They have pursued further a theme first explored by Rousseau — the problem of controlling the tendency towards an ever greater concentration of power in the hands of remote elites.

In one respect they are significantly like the democratic elitists whom they criticise. Both are pluralists. The radicals claim, however, that they seek to introduce participation into those areas which are most meaningful to the citizen – government and economic life – whilst in their view the intermediary groups favoured by their opponents – parent-teacher associations, clubs, churches and even unions – do not give access to the major sources of influence on people's lives. For 'radical democrats', as for Rousseau and Marx, whose work so often seems to be an inspiration to them, men who are deprived of responsibility and are not masters of their own lives are not fully-developed men. However benevolent and wise the elite its existence is no substitute for individual participation in social decision-making. On this view man develops himself and becomes a responsible, moral agent through the process of participation.

The two views of democracy and of the role of elites thus appear irreconcilable. It seems, at first sight, that men must choose between them. G. C. Field once offered a possible solution to the definitional problem of democracy when he said that a state is democratic "... not *if*, but *in so far* as the great mass of the population can exercise an effective influence on the decisions that make up the work of government".[35] It is true that this is a solution in which participation is the chief criterion but is the solution incapable of modification so as to form something approaching a common ground between the democratic elitists and the radical democrats? Radicals might wish to replace the word 'government' by something more general, whilst democratic elitists might query the appropriateness of 'mass'; but essentially, as the elitist thesis itself demonstrates, the crux is that there can be, and are, stronger and weaker versions of many political theories, among them democratic theory. Where popular influence is very weak (it is never totally absent) a regime can certainly be termed elitist; where it is very strong a system in which it is impossible for all members to take part in key decisions may still be called democratic. It may also be said of a society that it has elements of democracy but that it should be made more democratic by opening up its institutions to greater participation; or it could be said, as a classical republican might say, that a society is sufficiently democratic and should be balanced by an elitist element.

The argument can continue with the parties accepting a great deal of common language rather than, as seems characteristic of much of this debate between elitists and radical democrats, speaking past each other. In politics few issues are capable of being settled by anything akin to a mathematical proof. Politics is one of those areas of human life where what is at issue is often a matter of degree. But it is seldom a matter of *mere* degree.

NOTES

1   W. Kornhauser, *The Politics of Mass Society*, Routledge, London, 1960.

2   P. Bachrach. *The Theory of Democratic Elitism: a Critique*; Jack L. Walker, 'A Critique of the Elitist Theory of Democracy', *American Political Science Review*, LX.2, June 1966, pp. 285–295. Note Dahl's reply and Walker's rejoinder in the same issue.

3   Fourth edition, Allen and Unwin, London, 1954. See esp. Ch. 22.

4   By Bachrach, *The Theory of Democratic Elitism*, pp. 18–25. See also T. Bottomore, *Elites and Society*, Watts, London, 1964, Ch. 6.

5   *Capitalism, Socialism and Democracy*, p. 296. See also E. Schattschneider, *Party Government*, Farrar and Rinehart, New York, 1942.

6   *Capitalism, Socialism and Democracy*, p. 295.

7   See also G. Sartori, *Democratic Theory*, Wayne State University Press, Detroit, 1962, p. 77.

8   See above, p. 113.

9   *British Journal of Sociology*, Vol. I, No. 1–2, 1950. See also E. Shils, *The Torment of Secrecy*, Free Press, Glencoe, 1956.

10 *The Politics of Mass Society*, p. 77.

11 But see above, p. 102.

12 *Democratic Theory*, pp. 124–7.

13 *Democratic Theory*, pp. 118–9.

14 See above, Ch. 1 and below, p. 132.

15 *Democratic Theory*, pp. 75–7.

16 'The New Democracy', *Political Studies*, Vol. XI No. 2, June 1963, pp. 156–77.

17 Stanford University Press, Stanford, 1961.

18 Prentice-Hall, Englewood Cliffs, N.J., 1966.

19 Watts, London, 1964.

20 *American Political Science Review*, June 1966, pp. 285–95.

21 Little, Brown, Boston and Toronto, 1967.

22 *American Political Science Review*, June 1966, pp. 296–7, 305.

23 *Representative Government*. Blackwell edition, Oxford, 1946, cited.

24 *Representative Government*, p. 202.

25 *Representative Government*, p. 189.

26 *The Power Elite*, p. 317.

27 *Elites and Society*, Chs. VI and VII.

28 *The Theory of Democratic Elitism*, p. 96.

29 *The Decline of American Pluralism*, pp. 269–77.

30 See further R. Dahrendorf, 'On the Origin of Social Inequality', in P. Laslett and W. G. Runciman, *Philosophy, Politics and Society*, 2nd Series, Blackwell, Oxford, 1962, pp. 88–109.

31 See Bottomore, *Elites and Society*, pp. 135–6.

32 Kariel, *The Decline of American Pluralism*, pp. 268-70; *The Promise of Politics*, pp. 63–5.

33 See Lord James, *Education and Leadership*, Harrap, London, 1951. A satirical account will be found in M. Young, *The Rise of the Meritocracy 1870–2033*, Thames and Hudson, London, 1958.

34 *The Promise of Politics*, pp. 62–9.

35 *Political Theory*, Methuen, London, 1956, p. 93. Emphasis in the original.

| bibliography

The 'classic' texts of elitist thought are:

G. Mosca, *The Ruling Class* (ed. Livingston), McGraw-Hill, New York, 1939.

V. Pareto, *The Mind and Society*, Harcourt-Brace, New York, 1935; a convenient selection from Pareto's writings is *Vilfredo Pareto: Sociological Writings*, (ed. S. E. Finer), Pall Mall Press, London; Praeger, New York, 1966.

R. Michels, *Political Parties*, Free Press, Glencoe, Illinois, 1958.

J. Burnham, *The Managerial Revolution*, Putnam, New York and London, 1942.

C. Wright Mills, *The Power Elite*, Oxford University Press, New York, 1956.

The following works are recommended as introductions to the material covered in each chapter

Chapter one
T. Bottomore, *Elites and Society*, Watts, London, 1964; Basic Books, New York, 1965.

Chapter two
J. Burnham, *The Machiavellians*, John Day, New York, 1943.

J. H. Meisel (ed.), *Pareto and Mosca*, Prentice-Hall, Englewood Cliffs, New Jersey, 1965.

C. W. Cassinelli, 'The Law of Oligarchy', *American Political Science Review*, XLVII, 3, 1953, pp. 773–784.

Chapter three
S. F. Nadel, 'The Concept of Social Elites', *International Social Science Bulletin*, Vol. 8, 1956, pp. 413–424.

Chapter four
J. Blondel, *Voters, Parties and Leaders*, Penguin, Harmondsworth, 1963; Penguin, New York, 1964.

F. Hunter, *Community Power Structure*, Anchor Books, Garden City, New York, 1963.

R. A. Dahl, *Who Governs?*, Yale University Press, New Haven, 1961.

R. Presthus, *Men at the Top*, Oxford University Press, New York, 1964.

Chapter five

R. A. Dahl, *Modern Political Analysis*, Prentice-Hall, Englewood Cliffs, New Jersey, 1963.

P. Bachrach & M. Baratz, 'Two Faces of Power', *American Political Science Review*, LVI, 1962, pp. 947–952.

W. J. M. Mackenzie, *Politics and Social Science*, Penguin, Harmondsworth, 1967. 'Models of Collective Decision-Making', *Social Sciences: Problems and Orientations*, Mouton for UNESCO, The Hague, May 1968, pp. 356–370.

G. Parry, 'Elites and Polyarchies', *Journal of Commonwealth Political Studies*, IV, 3, Nov., 1966, pp. 163–179.

Chapter six

G. Sartori, *Democratic Theory*, Wayne State University Press, Detroit, 1962.

P. Bachrach, *The Theory of Democratic Elitism: a Critique*, Little, Brown, Boston and Toronto, 1967.

Other recommended reading:

S. Aaronovitch, *The Ruling Class*, Lawrence & Wishart, London, 1961.

Acton Society Trust, *Management Succession*, London, 1958.

R. Agger, D. Goldrich and B. Swanson, *The Rulers and the Ruled*, Wiley, New York, 1964.

V. L. Allen, *Power in Trade Unions*, Longmans, London, 1954.

G. A. Almond and S. Verba, *The Civic Culture*, Little, Brown, Boston and Toronto, 1965.

M. Anderson, 'The Myth of the 'Two Hundred Families'' *Political Studies*, XIII, 2, June, 1965, pp. 163–178.

H. Arendt, 'What is Authority?', *Between Past and Future*, Viking, New York; Faber, London, 1961.

J. Armstrong, *The Soviet Bureaucratic Elite*, Praeger, New York; Stevens, London, 1959.

R. Aron, 'Social Structure and the Ruling Class', *British Journal of Sociology*, I, nos. 1–2, 1950, pp. 1–16 and 126–143.

J. L. Austin, *How to do Things with Words*, Oxford University Press, London, 1962. 'Performative Utterances', *Philosophical Papers*, Oxford University Press, London, 1961, pp. 220–239.

W. Bagehot, *The English Constitution* (ed. Crossman), Fontana, London, 1963.

E. C. Banfield, *Political Influence*, Free Press, New York, 1961.

M. Barratt-Brown, 'The Controllers', *Universities and Left Review*, Autumn, 1958, pp. 53–61.

B. Barry, *Political Argument*, Routledge, London, 1965.

G. Belknap and R. Smuckler, 'Political Power Relations in a Mid-West City', *Public Opinion Quarterly*, Spring, 1956, pp. 73–81.

R. Bendix, *Max Weber*, Heinemann, London; Doubleday, New York, 1960.

A. F. Bentley, *The Process of Government*, Principia Press, Bloomington, 1949.

A. A. Berle and G. C. Means, *The Modern Corporation and Private Property*, Macmillan, New York, 1932.

T. Bishop and R. Wilkinson, *Winchester and the Public School Elite*, Faber, London, 1967.

S. Brittan, *The Treasury under the Tories, 1951–1964*, Penguin, Harmondsworth, 1964.

J. M. Buchanan and G. Tullock, *The Calculus of Consent*, University of Michigan Press, Ann Arbor, 1962.

H. Channon, *Chips: The Diaries of Sir Henry Channon*, Weidenfeld and Nicolson, London, 1967.

D. Clark, *The Industrial Manager*, Business Publications, London, 1966.

R. V. Clements, *Managers*, Allen and Unwin, London, 1958.

G. H. Copeman, *Leaders of British Industry*, Gee, London, 1955.

G. A. Craig, *The Politics of the Prussian Army*, Oxford University Press. Galaxy Books, New York, 1964.

R. A. Dahl and C. E. Lindblom, *Politics, Economics, and Welfare*, Harper, New York, 1953.

R. A. Dahl, 'A Critique of the Ruling Elite Model', *American Political Science Review*, Vol. LII, 1958, pp. 463–469.

    A Preface to Democratic Theory, Phoenix edition, Chicago, 1963. 'The City in the Future of Democracy', *American Political Science Review*, LXI, 4, 1967, pp. 953–970.

R. Dahrendorf, 'On the Origin of Social Inequality', in P. Laslett and W, G. Runciman, *Philosophy, Politics and Society*, 2nd series, Blackwell, Oxford, 1962, pp. 88–109.

A. V. Dicey, *Law and Public Opinion in England during the Nineteenth Century*, Macmillan, London, 1905.

C. H. Dodd, 'Recruitment to the Administrative Class 1960–64', *Public Administration*, Spring 1967, pp. 55–80.

A. Downs, *An Economic Theory of Democracy*, Harper and Row, New York, 1957.

G. Duncan and S. Lukes, 'The New Democracy', *Political Studies*, XI, 2, June, 1963. pp. 156–177.

L. J. Edinger & D. D. Searing, 'Social Background in Elite Analysis: A Methodological Inquiry', *American Political Science Review*, LXI, 2, June, 1967. pp. 428–445.

P. Ferris, *The City*, Penguin, Harmondsworth, 1962.

G. C. Field, *Political Theory*, Methuen, London; Barnes & Noble, New York, 1956.

S. E. Finer, 'The Political Power of Private Capital', *The Sociological Review*, III, 1955, pp. 279–294 and IV, 1956, pp. 5–30.

    The Man on Horseback, Pall Mall Press, London; Praeger, New York, 1962.

P. Sargent Florence, *Ownership, Control and Success of Large Companies*, Sweet and Maxwell, London, 1961.

C. J. Friedrich, *Man and His Government*, McGraw-Hill, New York, 1963.

D. Granick, *The European Executive*, Doubleday, Garden City, New York, 1962.

W. L. Guttsman, *The British Political Elite*, Macgibbon and Kee, London, 1963.

H. L. A. Hart, *The Concept of Law*, Oxford University Press, London, 1961.

C. Hill, 'The Norman Yoke', *Puritanism and Revolution*, Secker and Warburg, London, 1958.

T. Hobbes, *Leviathan*.

R. Hofstadter, *The Paranoid Style in American Politics*, Knopf, New York, 1966.

Lord James, *Education and Leadership*, Harrap, London, 1951.

M. Janowitz, *The Professional Soldier*, Free Press of Glencoe, New York, 1960.

T. Jones, *A Diary with Letters, 1931–1950*, Oxford University Press, London, 1964.

H. S. Kariel, *The Decline of American Pluralism*, Stanford University Press, Stanford, 1961.

    The Promise of Politics, Prentice-Hall, Englewood Cliffs, New Jersey, 1966.

S. Keller, *Beyond the Ruling Class*, Random House, New York, 1963.

R. Kelsall, *Higher Civil Servants in Britain*, Routledge, London, 1955.

W. Kornhauser, *The Politics of Mass Society*, The Free Press, Glencoe, Ill., 1959; Routledge, London, 1960.

V. I. Lenin, *What Is To Be Done?*

R. Lewis and R. Stewart, *The Boss*, Phoenix House, London, 1958.

S. M. Lipset and A. Solari (eds), *Elites in Latin America*, Oxford University Press, New York, 1967.

T. Lupton and C. S. Wilson, 'The Social Background and Connections of 'Top Decision Makers'', *Manchester School*, XXVII, 1959, pp. 30–51.

K. Marx, *Selected Writings in Sociology and Social Philosophy* (ed. Bottomore and Rubel), Watts, London, 1956.

    The Eighteenth Brumaire of Louis Bonaparte, Marx and Engels Selected Works, Vol. I, Lawrence and Wishart, London, 1958.

J. D. May, 'Democracy, Organization, Michels', *American Political Science Review*, LIX, 2, June, 1965, pp. 417–429.

R. T. McKenzie, *British Political Parties*, Heinemann, London; St. Martins Press, New York, 1955.

J. S. Mill, *Representative Government*, Blackwell, Oxford, 1946; Oxford University Press, New York.

C. Wright Mills, *The Sociological Imagination*, Oxford University Press, New York, 1959, Evergreen edition, New York, 1961.

    The New Men of Power, Harcourt-Brace, New York, 1948.

G. Mosca, *Histoire des doctrines politiques*, Payot, Paris, 1936.

J. P. Nettl, 'Consensus or Elite Domination: The Case of Business', *Political Studies*, XIII, I, February, 1965, pp. 22-44.

H. Nicolson, *Harold Nicolson: Diaries and Letters, 1939-1945*, Collins, London, 1967.

M. Oakeshott, 'Political Education', *Rationalism in Politics*, Methuen, London; Basic Books, New York, 1962.

M. Ostrogorski, *Democracy and The Organization of Political Parties*, Macmillan, London, 1902.

B. Page, D. Leitch and P. Knightly, *Philby: The Spy Who Betrayed a Generation*, Deutsch, London, 1968; issued as *The Philby Conspiracy*, Doubleday, New York, 1968.

H. Parris, 'Twenty Years of l'Ecole Nationale d'Administration', *Public Administration*, 43, 1965, pp. 395-411.

T. Parsons, *The Structure of Social Action*, Free Press, Glencoe, 1949.

P. E. P., 'Government by Appointment', *Planning*, XXVI, No. 443, Political and Economic Planning, London, 1960.
  Advisory Committees in British Government, Political and Economic Planning, London, 1960.

N. W. Polsby, *Community Power and Political Theory*, Yale University Press, New Haven, 1963.

J. Porter, *The Vertical Mosaic*, University of Toronto Press, Toronto, 1965.

A. Potter, *Organized Groups in British National Politics*, Faber, London, 1961.
  'The American Governing Class', *British Journal of Sociology*, XIII, 4, December 1962, pp. 309-319.

G. Prezzolini, 'L'aristocrazia dei briganti', from *Il Regno*, 1903, reprinted in *La Cultura italiana del '900 attraverso le reviste*, vol. I, 1960.

F. F. Ridley, 'French Technocracy and Comparative Government', *Political Studies*, XIV, 1, February 1966, pp. 34-52.

A. M. Rose, *The Power Structure*, Oxford University Press, Galaxy Books, New York, 1967.

R. Rose, *Politics in England*, Little, Brown, Boston and Toronto, 1964.

W. G. Runciman, *Social Science and Political Theory*, Cambridge University Press, London, 1963.
  Relative Deprivation and Social Justice, Routledge, London, 1966.

A. Sampson, *Anatomy of Britain*, Hodder and Stoughton, London; Harper, New York, 1962.
  Anatomy of Britain Today, Hodder and Stoughton, London; Harper, New York, 1965.

E. Schattschneider, *Party Government*, Farrar and Rinehart, New York, 1942.

R. O. Schulze and L. U. Blumberg, 'The Determination of Local Power Elites', *American Journal of Sociology*, November, 1957, pp. 290-6.

J. Schumpeter, *Capitalism, Socialism and Democracy*, Harper, New York, 1956; Allen and Unwin, 4th edition, London, 1954.

R. E. Scott, 'Political Elites and Political Modernization: The Crisis of Transition', in S. M. Lipset and A. Solari, *Elites in Latin America*, Oxford University Press, New York, 1967, pp. 117–145

E. Shils, *The Torment of Secrecy*, Free Press, Glencoe, Ill., 1956

P. Thoenes, *The Elite in the Welfare State*, Faber, London, 1966.

History of The Times, vol. IV, Pt. II, The Times, London, 1952.

D. Truman, *The Governmental Process*, Knopf, New York, 1951.

R. H. Turner, 'Sponsored and Contest Mobility and the School System', *American Sociological Review*, December, 1960, pp. 855–867.

T. Veblen, *The Theory of the Leisure Class*, Macmillan, 1899, republished Mentor Books, 1953.

A. J. Vidich and J. Bensman, *Small Town in Mass Society*, Princeton University Press, Princeton, 1958.

G. Wallas, *Human Nature in Politics*, Constable, London, 1908.

J. Walker, 'A Critique of the Elitist Theory of Democracy', *American Political Science Review*, LX, 1966, pp. 285–295.

W. L. Warner and J. C. Abegglen, *Big Business Leaders in America*, Harper, New York, 1955.

S. & B. Webb, *Industrial Democracy*, Longmans, London, 1897.

M. Weber, *From Max Weber* (eds Gerth and Mills), Routledge, London, 1957.

H. H. Wilson, *Pressure Group*, Secker and Warburg, London, 1961.

K. Wittfogel, *Oriental Despotism*, Yale University Press, New Haven, 1957.

S. Wolin, *Politics and Vision*, Little, Brown, Boston, 1960; Allen and Unwin, London, 1961.

G. Wrench, *Geoffrey Dawson and our Times*, Hutchinson, London, 1955.

M. Young, *The Rise of the Meritocracy*, Thames & Hudson, London, 1958.

|index

www.ingramcontent.com/pod-product-compliance
Lightning Source LLC
Chambersburg PA
CBHW050528270326
41926CB00015B/3122